# HEAVEN SENT

## MARY ANN MCRANEY

Copyright © 2015 by Mary Ann McRaney

*HEAVEN SENT*
by Mary Ann McRaney

Printed in the United States of America.

ISBN 9781498438025

All rights reserved solely by the author. The author guarantees all contents are original and do not infringe upon the legal rights of any other person or work. No part of this book may be reproduced in any form without the permission of the author. The views expressed in this book are not necessarily those of the publisher.

Unless otherwise indicated, Scripture quotations taken from the King James Version (KJV) – *public domain*.

www.xulonpress.com

THIS BOOK IS DEDICATED
TO MY SON, JAMIE.

Therefore angels are only servants ... sent to care for people who will inherit salvation.
Hebrews 1: 14

"For I know the plans I have for you," says the Lord. "They are plans for good and not for disaster, to give you a future and a hope. In those days when you pray, I will listen. If you look for me wholeheartedly, you will find me."
Jeremiah 29: 11-13

# CHAPTER ONE

The moon bathed the narrow Mississippi country road with soft light. The red Ford Ranger was traveling at a high rate of speed; the driver preoccupied with his own thoughts. The windows of the small truck were rolled down, and the humid night air enveloped the teenager like a moist cocoon. He paid no attention to the landscape that barely registered in his mind's eye as he pushed the gas pedal harder. Pine tree after pine tree lined the road like silent sentinels as the truck sped by. Occasionally, the tree line would break for a field encased with fence posts and barbed wire. He had seen it all many times before. This was his way home.

Josh Stewart was late. He was preoccupied with making up the lies he would tell his parents when he got home. The truth was that after football practice which had lasted all morning, he and his teammates had made their way to the local swimming hole to cool off. It was the last day of preseason practice before school started on Monday. It had been two weeks of strenuous hell in unbearable heat and humidity that south Mississippi was famous for.

It had been his usual crew of friends who whooped and hollered as they swung from the rope tied to an overhanging tree to splash into the cool water of the small meandering stream that ran through their county until it fed into a larger tributary that eventually emptied into the Gulf of Mexico. It was a place they all knew well and had been a gathering place since childhood. Raucous laughter and plenty of smack talk was being bantered around as the guys talked about the football schedule and the new school year ahead. His teammates had been Josh's best buds since elementary school and made up the core of the football team. They were at the top of the food chain in the high school they attended, the jocks that everyone looked up to and wanted to be like. It was an enviable place to be for any high school boy, so why did Josh often wish he was just a nobody and not part of this elite group. Ah, the answer to that question only made his foot press harder on the accelerator of his truck.

After cooling off at the swimming hole, the gang had made their way back to the football locker room for showers and a change of clothes. Coach Barnes was still there in his office doing paperwork and drawing plays in his strategy book. He lived for the game and expected his boys to give a hundred percent during practice as well as on game night. Coach was a man to fear when you weren't giving it your all on the playing field, yet he understood the need for his boys to blow off steam and have some recreation time. He fully understood that boys will be boys and most of the time looked the other way when his team was rough housing or pulling some juvenile prank in the locker

## Chapter One

room. All he really cared about was winning on Friday nights because a winning season kept his job secure.

He knew the boys, after they cleaned up, would be heading over to the back- to- school party hosted by head cheerleader, Mandy Sims. He also knew that Mandy's parents were out of town. Her father was the bank president and a loyal booster club member. He and his wife were on a business trip to New Orleans. Coach Barnes shrugged to himself. It wasn't his place to police what Mandy Sims did while her parents were away. He good-naturedly waved the boys off with encouragement to have a good time, thinking about his own youthful exploits on and off the football field back in the day.

And yes indeed, their little close knit clique had a great time at Mandy's party. Why wouldn't they? They ruled the universe, didn't they? Everybody that was somebody at the high school was there. The kegs were flowing, the cute girls were vying for any boy's attention they could get, and no parents to cramp their style. That's right! No, parents, no chaperones, Mandy had the whole place to do whatever she wanted, and she wanted to throw the most righteous party ever. What a great way to start this school year off in style.

Mandy and her boyfriend Skip Davis were seniors. Skip, the quarterback of the football team, had it all, handsome, smart, with a body any girl would drool over. Mandy, who was fiercely jealous, keep him on a short leash. There were a few other couples within their little group, but most of the guys were on the prowl for anything the girls were willing to give out. The only rule was to stay within the perimeter of the clique, the football players and the cheerleaders and a few selected others deemed good enough to socialize with. If you didn't fit the criteria, you sure as hell weren't getting in the group. There were always the wannabees, who tried to get in, but were promptly put in their place usually in some humiliating manner.

Josh ran his fingers through his windblown hair, then slammed his clenched fist against the steering wheel. He despised the limits his own group of friends had enforced on him. Why did it have to be that way, their way, or nothing. He had left the party early, leaving his buddies behind to enjoy themselves. The drinking was getting out of hand as usual, and the hookups were starting to find their way to the empty bedrooms. He had made up some excuse about his dad needing him the next morning bright and early. It was a lie because he hadn't gone straight home.

He made his way back to the now deserted swimming hole. He parked his truck on an embankment overlooking the water. He reached under the dashboard of his vehicle and found the plastic bag he had taped there. He stuffed the bag in his shirt pocket, got out of the truck, slid down the embankment, found a comfortable spot close to the overhanging tree, and settled down. Then he fished the bag out of his pocket, opened it, reached in for the marijuana joint, put it in his mouth, and after fumbling with getting the lighter out of the bag, lit up, and took a deep drag.

He blew the smoke out slowly savoring the first hit. He took another drag and felt his muscles start to relax. Sitting there looking at the moonlight dance over the water, listening to the sounds of the night

## Chapter One

especially the loud high pitched noise the crickets made, Josh didn't have a care in the world. Another lie, but that's why he loved pot. It made you forget for a little while. You didn't care about a damn thing while you were smoking weed. What a great escape, temporarily of course.

This was the part he would have to lie to his parents about. They wouldn't care about his hanging out with friends at the swimming hole or even being at the party although they had no idea that parents wouldn't be there. You see, Josh's parents trusted him. He had never failed to make curfew which was one o'clock on the weekend. Some of his buddies could stay out later, but he was ok with his own time limit. It was his own private party with Mary Jane that he would have to cover up with lies to his parents.

He leaned back in the cool grass, inhaling deeply. His parents would be freaked out if they could see him now. They were good southern Christian people who expected a lot out of their only child. He could hear them in his head harping on the dangers of marijuana, sure to lead him down the wrong path to a depraved useless life. Really, he thought as he glanced at his watch to check the time. Where do parents get such crazy information?

Josh sat up, looking at his watch again. He could barely make out the time using the moonlight to illuminate the face of the new wrist watch his parents had given him for his sixteenth birthday last month. He hated having a late summer birthday. It made him one of the youngest people in his class. He was just starting his junior year at sixteen when many of his classmates would be turning seventeen during the school year. That was the pits! He glanced at his watch again. He had twenty minutes to get home; he better get a move on. His parents would already be in bed, but his mother would not be asleep, not until he came home.

Josh stood up, stamping out the butt of the joint in the sand before kicking it into the water. He gave a deep sigh watching it slowly float downstream before he made his way up to the truck. After getting in, he secured the baggie back underneath his dash, cranked the truck, and headed home. Backing up, he took a good look at himself in the rear view mirror. His dirty blond hair was damp from the humid night air. Blue-gray eyes were slightly bloodshot from the joint he had just smoked. He stared deep into the eyes of the boy in the mirror. He didn't like what he saw there. Liar, pot smoker, slacker, his parents would be devastated to know he was smoking weed on a regular basis. They'd never understand his need for it, never in a million years. He flipped the mirror around so he couldn't see his reflection.

That's how he found himself speeding down the country road with the windows rolled down, and the warm night air blowing through his truck. He was alone with his thoughts, thoughts that were turning toward the dark side. A soft voice seemed to be whispering in his ear, loser, drug user, reject, misfit. He shook his head to try and stop those words from rolling around in his head. He wasn't that bad, was he? A real despondency gripped him. What kind of life was he going to have if all of those words were true? How

## Chapter One

much pain would he cause his parents if he didn't live up to their expectations? Who were his real friends? Could he stop smoking joints cold turkey, or did he really want to? What was wrong with him? Thoughts were running through his head as fast as the small truck was flying down the narrow road.

Josh knew he was coming upon a dangerous curve in the road soon. That voice in his head whispered an intriguing thought. Just a tug on the steering wheel in that curve would send the truck barreling into a thicket of pine trees that stood thirty or forty feet away from the road. No one would ever know. Everyone would think it was a terrible accident. Why not? Then all your troubles would be over, loser. The seductive voice kept whispering in his ear.

The sixteen year old seemed confused. Whose voice was that anyway? Was it his own dark thoughts or an evil presence egging him on? As he neared the curve, the truck accelerated as his foot pressed the gas pedal down, and his headlights pierced the darkness to illuminate the large, tall pine trees a short distance from the road. He didn't seem in control anymore. The voice in his head wanted to know if he would do it. A trickle of sweat rolled down his forehead. The voice whispered in his ear one last time. "Come on, Josh, don't be a woose, a wimp, a coward. DO IT!"

With those words reverberating in his head, Josh Stewart's right hand jerked the steering wheel of his truck so that it left the road in the middle of the curve and was headed straight for the stand of trees. In a split second, he came to his senses and jerked the wheel back to the left which caused the vehicle to start skidding sideways along the shoulder of the road. He tried his best to regain control of the truck before it slammed into the trees looming closer and closer. He slammed on the brakes, gave the wheel one last forceful jerk back toward the road, closed his eyes, and braced for the impact, which never came. The truck came to an abrupt stop just a few feet away from the tall pine trees. Somehow he had narrowly avoided an accident that certainly could have killed him.

He sat there shaken, barely able to comprehend what just happened. Tears welled up in his eyes. Confusion swirled around him. He had listened to that voice and its seductive whispers and had almost ended his life on this lonely stretch of country road. He was sixteen year old and had just stared death in the face. Was he mentally deranged? What was wrong with him? He clenched his fist and pounded it on the dash. The tears began to flow down his cheeks. He put his face in his hands and leaned his head down until it rested on the steering wheel. He felt the darkness of the night, the loneliness of the isolated road, the heaviness of the humid air, and the horror of what had almost happened press in on him until he felt like he had the weight of the whole world on his shoulders.

Josh Stewart didn't know what to do, but he did know someone who had the answers he needed. He lifted his head, his gaze peering through the windshield into the night sky where the moon was brightly glowing. Then it was his turn to whisper softly, "God, please help me."

## CHAPTER TWO

"Gabriella," God's thunderous voice reverberated across heaven. The young angel quickened her pace as she hurried toward the majestic building that housed the throne of God. She barely glanced in the direction of the towering avenging angel who stood at attention with his flaming sword held out in front of him. This was the third time she had been summoned by God himself. She wasn't as overwhelmed by her surroundings as she had been in the past; however, the love of God flooded every particle of her being as she stepped in His presence. "Awesome! God is so awesome!" were the thoughts that filled her head.

As her eyes adjusted to the brilliant light radiating from His Holiness, she realized she wasn't the only one in His presence. Kneeling in front of His throne was a magnificent angel who was emitting a powerful glowing radiance. His handsome face was surrounded by golden hair that reached his shoulders. His piercing blue eyes were the color of the bluest sky. His powerful body was dressed in white linen which had been interwoven with finely spun gold to create a shimmering effect whenever he moved. He had a golden belt around his waist and attached to the belt was a golden ring with large golden keys dangling from it. On his feet were golden sandals.

Gabriella stood rooted to the spot as she saw the hand of God slowly come forth from the brilliant light that surrounded His throne. The mighty hand of God descended onto the kneeling angel's shoulder and rested there. The angel lifted his bowed head and gazed deeply into the light. God's voice, not so thunderous now, spoke lovingly, "Well done my faithful archangel. Well done indeed, Gabriel."

Gabriella gasped. Gabriel? Could this possibly be her namesake, the archangel Gabriel? He was the messenger of God who from the beginning of time had given mankind divine communications from their Creator. Why everyone knew it was this very angel who had appeared to the virgin Mary to tell her that she was to be the mother of Jesus, the Son of God.

He was a legend among all the other angels. His exploits were well-documented in the holy book. He was much talked about but seldom seen because he was ever busy on the earth with God's most important business. Gabriella's gaze fell on the golden keys dangling from the archangel's belt. The keys of God's kingdom were for His children on the earth. When revelation or knowledge of these keys was released to those who belonged to God, they excelled in everything they did, accomplishing great deeds on the earth. The holy book was filled with stories of such deeds done by men and women who glorified God with their faith motivated actions. The wondrous feats of angels were also recorded throughout the Bible to remind mankind of the supernatural help they have when needed. The heavenly host of angels often wondered why more people on the earth didn't seek out this mystery of the keys because Father God longed to release wisdom and understanding of His kingdom to all who sought Him for it.

Gabriella inhaled deeply as she saw the hand of God lift from Gabriel's shoulder and motion for His other archangel to step forward. In his hands, Michael held a rolled-up scroll bound together with golden thread. This scroll was much larger than the ones Gabriella had been given from the Room of Souls before she had been sent on her earthly assignments. Obviously, this was kingdom business of a much larger scale involving many people over a larger area. Michael broke the red seal of the Lamb and opened the scroll giving one end to Gabriel so that both could study the contents. What a magnificent pair they made standing there side by side. The young angel could barely believe she was witnessing such an awesome sight. She didn't dare disturb them.

As the two poured over the contents of the scroll, Gabriella took time to savor this experience. Even though she had been in this very sanctuary twice before, she breathed deeply in the presence of Holy God. Light and love permeated every molecule in this place. As the heavenly chorus swirled around His throne singing " Holy, Holy, Holy," Gabriella wanted to join in the worship for the Creator of all things. Energy pulsated in, around, and through the room just like the living water that flowed under the glass floor and cascaded in a waterfall at the foot of His throne. Yet, the two archangels seemed unmoved by their glorious surrounding. They were intent on the scroll, speaking softly to each other, sometimes pointing at what was written on the ancient parchment paper.

Then the discussion was over. The scroll was rolled back up. Gabriel and Michael both knelt before the throne of God. Even though she couldn't see God's face because of the brilliant light emitting from it, Gabriella could feel that God was smiling for He was well-pleased with these two mighty archangels. As they stood, God's voice spoke to only one of them. "GO, GABRIEL, MY MESSENGER, AND DO MY WILL UPON THE EARTH."

The archangel quickly took his leave and almost ran right in to the young angel standing near the door. He stopped and with a smile of recognition said, "Why it's my little namesake, Gabriella. I've been hearing good things about you, my little one."

Gabriella could hardly believe her ears. She tried to sputter out a reply, but the only thing that escaped her throat was a high-pitched squeak.

"Yes," he continued, "I know all about your assignments, two very difficult ones to be sure, but excellently executed for a young angel just beginning her eternal purpose. Keep up the good work, my little Gabby. I'm off just now on a very important mission that involves the leaders of several nations who must be made aware of God's plans, but we will meet again, I promise you." With that goodbye, he hurried on his way.

## Chapter Two

"Gabby, he called me Gabby," was what stuck in her mind. That was the name her human assignments used. He knew about them too, Cassie, Jessica, who were not just her assignments on earth, but her dear, dear friends. The mighty archangel Gabriel had complimented her on the good job she had done. Could any angel in heaven be as happy as she was?

She turned her attention to Michael, who was still standing by the throne of God. Who would her assignment be this time? He motioned for her to come closer. As she did, he pulled a scroll from the pocket of his robe and held it out to her. The scroll looked just like the two previous ones, yet the archangel had a peculiar look on his face as he placed it in her hand. He started to say something but shrugged his shoulders and turned away to take his place in front of the door that led to the Room of Souls.

It was God's voice that came next. "GABRIELLA, GO AND DO MY WILL ON THE EARTH."

And because of the archangel Gabriel's words of encouragement, Gabriella had the courage to do something she had never done before. As she knelt before His throne, she spoke to God, the One who was, who is, and will always be from everlasting to everlasting. In a quivering voice, she said, "Yes, Lord."

The magnitude of speaking to God overwhelmed the young angel, and she made her way out of the throne room on trembling legs. "Wow!" she spoke her thoughts out loud. "It couldn't possibly get any better than what I just experienced. The archangel Gabriel spoke to me, and I spoke to God Almighty."

She joyfully skipped down the street of pure gold basking in her divine experience. She loved being God's servant sent to help His children on the earth. She turned her attention to the scroll in her hand and quickly opened it anxious to read about her next assignment. Her eyes skimmed though the written words down to the name. She wanted to know the name. Cassie had been first, then Jessica, and now who would be next. She would read the entire document as soon as she found out the name.

There it was at the bottom of the scroll, Joshua Stewart. Gabriella couldn't believe her eyes at first, but there was his name. His name, she laughed out loud and threw the scroll high up into the air. She twirled around in excitement. Her next assignment was a boy!

# CHAPTER THREE

The first day of school was always hectic and confusing. Dazed students still in summer mode were milling about the hallways looking for lockers and classrooms that matched their printed out schedules. Whittleton High was a small high school in a small town. The ninth through twelfth grades had approximately five hundred students. The school had four wings, one for each grade level, attached to a main complex of administrative offices with a cafeteria and gymnasium across a courtyard dotted with benches and tables for students. Breezeways connected each hallway with each other as well as the office complex.

The school was located at the south end of town where there was plenty of room for the football stadium and adjacent field house. Like most small towns, football was big in Whittleton. Friday nights found most residents filling the bleachers ready to cheer for the home team.

Football practice was on Josh Stewart's mind as he stood by his locker talking to his best friend Kyle Jarvis. They had been best buds since kindergarten, yet they couldn't be more different, Josh, the tall stocky football linebacker, and Kyle, the wisecracking jokester.

Josh let out his frustration. "It'll be a hundred degrees in the shade, man, and Coach Barnes will make us practice till we drop. I hate it! Sweating like a pig and smelling like one too. See what you're missing, bud."

"Yeah, dude, I must be out of my freaking mind to miss all that," Kyle sarcastically replied. "Hey, I'm smart enough not to play sports. Who wants to get their brains raddled by some jerk in a jersey? No offense, dude. So suck it up and just enjoy the adoration of all your fans, almighty Whittleton jock. Say can I carry your books to your next class, master of the universe? It would be my honor." He bowed deeply.

"Knock it off, Kyle." Josh was not amused by his friend's banter.

Just then Kyle let out a low whistle followed by, "Hey, catch a look at what just walked through the doors of the eleventh grade hallway."

Josh turned around slightly curiously about what had caught his friend's attention, and there she stood. His heart literally skipped a beat or two before he swallowed hard to try and control the fluttery feeling in his chest that was now in his stomach also.

Kyle, completely unaware of his friend's reaction, commented, "Well, looky here. We got us a new chick on the block. Wonder what those high and mighty cheerleaders are going to think about her?"

Josh hadn't heard a word. He was staring at the new girl. She had stopped just inside the double doors. She was looking around obviously trying to take in

## Chapter Three

her new surroundings. She had on blue jeans with a multi-colored floral top. Her brown slightly curly hair was pulled back from her face and tied loosely with a ribbon. She had a friendly smile on her face and a deep dimple in her right cheek. Her large blue eyes were rimmed with dark full lashes. She wasn't a beauty, but there was definitely something about her that made you look twice. She had a book bag slung over her shoulder.

Just then everyone had their attention diverted by a commotion a few feet away. A ninth grader, hopelessly lost on the first day of school, had found his way into the eleventh grade hallway, and the upper classmen were having some fun.

The bigger boys were calling the young kid names and bumping in to him on purpose. His face was a mask of fear as he tried to navigate through the throng of students. One of the guys, a member of the football team, actually grabbed the kid's book bag and sent it flying across the floor spilling out his school supplies to the raucous laughter of all who were watching.

The new girl's smile was quickly replaced with a look of compassion for the frightened boy. As he scrambled around on the floor trying to retrieve his supplies, she knelt down beside him to help.

Josh, who had been watching with everyone else, slowly maneuvered his way to the two people on the floor. He squatted down next to the ninth grader and managed to stuff everything back into his book bag as the new girl handed it to him. Then he hauled the kid up, placed the bag on his shoulders, and pointed him in the direction he needed to go to rejoin his grade level.

The boy could barely whisper thanks before he hurried out the door.

"Hi. I'm Josh, which is short for Joshua."

"I'm Gabriella, but my friends call me Gabby."

Now that Josh was closer, he thought to himself. There's something unusual about this girl. Her face seemed to light up when she smiled, and there was almost like a twinkle in her eyes too.

"Ugh, can I help you find anything, your locker maybe or your first period class?"

Gabby flashed that smile again. "That would be great." She glanced at her schedule. "It's locker 214."

"That will be down the hall a ways. It's not too far from mime. I've got 224."

They stopped in front of her locker.

"What's your first period class?"

After referring to her schedule again, Gabby answered, "Algebra II with Mr. Kingsford."

Josh gave a loud groan. "I hate math. I'm not any good at it, but Mr. Kingsford is a pretty good teacher. I've got English first. I hate that even more than math. I'm not good at English either."

"What are you good at, Josh?" Gabby asked with a serious look on her face.

He looked deeply into her eyes then shrugged his shoulders. "I don't know; I haven't figured it out yet."

They continued walking until they stopped in front of the classroom. With a wave of his hand, Josh said, "Well, here you are at Algebra II. I'm sure I'll see you later in the day, Gabby. We have a small class. Everybody knows each other. All of our classes are in this wing." He was rambling not wanting the

*Chapter Three*

conversation to end and finally added, "I hope your first day at Whittleton High is a great one." That sounded a little goofy. He gave her a sheepish smile.

"Thank you for all your help, Josh. See you later."

They parted ways as Gabby entered the classroom, and Josh kept walking down the hall to his first period class. Kyle came up behind him and whispered, "That was smooth, dude, real smooth. You put the moves on the new girl as soon as she got in the door. I'm proud of you, Joshie boy. You're not usually such a player when it comes to the ladies. What's so different about this chick?"

Josh ignored his friend as he turned the corner and entered English class. He took a seat in the back of the room next to the windows. He frequently gazed out of the windows instead of giving what was going on in the classroom his undivided attention. His grades suffered for it, but he didn't care. That was a lie. He did care, only because it was a source of disappointment to his parents who expected better grades from him. He hated it when he disappointed anyone.

He thought back to Kyle's question and didn't know the answer. What was different about the new girl? He couldn't put his finger on it, but he knew she was different, special somehow. He could feel it deep down inside of himself where he had never felt anything like it before. Heck, back in the hallway when he first saw her, it was practically like an out of body experience. Weird he thought, but he also knew without a doubt that meeting Gabby today was one of those rare important occurrences that he would remember for the rest of his life.

# Chapter Four

He was already seated at the jocks' table in the cafeteria. The members of the football team came through the door and went down the food line in a group. It had a powerful effect on the student body. All eyes were on them, the privileged elite of the school. They laughed and joked with each other, ignoring anyone who wasn't in their inner circle. The lunch ladies always put more food on their trays while making eye contact and smiling like giddy teenagers, all because the studs on the team were coming through the cafeteria line.

Then the jocks would make their way to the two best tables in the cafeteria situated in the back corner. It was there they would hold court with their respective girlfriends who clung to their boyfriends with desperate fierceness. Some of the guys on the team had steady ladies who had been placed on a pedestal almost as high as the athlete they were dating. It was a place every girl wanted to be, and no girl was going to give up without a fight.

## Chapter Four

Josh had managed to avoid that particular pitfall. He had several friends that were girls, but that was it. Some of the guys liked to play the field, score as many touchdowns as possible without a steady girlfriend to tie them down. Josh wasn't one of them though. He was waiting. Waiting for what he wasn't exactly sure, but he was waiting. His teammates didn't get it and mercilessly teased him about it. Then there were the girls who tried to get close to him, letting him know they would do anything he wanted to do. It was tempting for sure, and he had almost given in several times to the urges that every teenage boy had. But something inside of him held back. He couldn't even really explain it, but he knew the first time was supposed to be special. So all those girls trying to give it away for free just got frustrated with Josh, but everybody agreed he was a good guy.

Yep, a good guy. That was his reputation, squeaky clean. Nobody seated at the table with him would believe this good guy had deliberately run his truck off the road the night before. That his truck had been headed for a thicket of pine trees before he lost the nerve to finish the job. He wondered if anyone else at the table had voices whispering condemnation in their heads telling them to end it all. Josh stared at his plate of lasagna. He was brought out of his dark thoughts when he heard a teammate comment.

"Whoa now, I wouldn't mind a piece of that."

"Yeah, fresh meat, baby," was yet another comment.

Josh looked up and saw the object of their attention, Gabby. She had just come through the cafeteria doors with, he groaned to himself, with a bunch of losers. What was her problem? She had only been at this school for a few hours, and she had managed to find the most unattractive girls, geeks, and misfits to eat lunch with. They were laughing and talking like they didn't have a care in the world. Gabby's dimple was clearly visible as she smiled, her face aglow with a light from within. Josh stared mesmerized, and again he could feel this spark of something deep inside that he didn't understand.

"That's the new girl," said Mandy. "I had her in my second period class. Looks like I'll have to straighten her out. Can you imagine hanging with that bunch of rejects?"

Everyone at the table voiced their agreement.

Skip, Mandy's quarterback boyfriend, drawled, "Honey, you just bring her right on in to our little private club. We need some new pickings, right dudes."

That comment was followed by some loud snickering and cat calls. Mandy's face flushed beet red, and some other girls who overheard the exchange giggled nervously.

Mandy leaned her head on her boyfriend's shoulder and put her hand on his thigh and squeezed hard. "Now, Skipper, you know I'm all you can handle, don't you?" The two looked knowingly at each other, and everyone at the table squealed with raucous laughter.

Josh shook his head and grimaced. Why, he thought, did everything always have to come down to sex. Being a teenager was difficult enough. Why did sex have to be thrown into the mix? He knew he was

## Chapter Four

one of the few guys who wasn't indulging in sexual satisfaction with girls who were more than willing to oblige. What was wrong with him? Oh yeah, he was waiting for something or someone, right? He glanced again to where Gabby sat surrounded by her interesting choice of lunch companions. He could tell by her friendly relaxed demeanor that she was very comfortable with her new friends. There was no hint of superiority or condemnation coming from her blue eyes. She laughed easily and was really interested in what her tablemates had to say. She wasn't looking around the cafeteria to see who she could see or be seen as so many others did.

However, she did glance up once to meet Josh's gaze across the room. She gave him a bright smile before she turned back to listen to the girl sitting next to her.

That smile had the oddest effect on Josh. He had never felt this way before. Maybe waiting was going to pay off after all because, maybe just maybe, he had found who he had been waiting for!

# CHAPTER FIVE

When the bell rang to signal lunch was over, Josh picked up his tray and made his way over to Gabby's table.

"What do you have for fourth period," he asked.

"U.S. History with Mr. Derry," was her reply without looking at her schedule.

"That's great cause that's my fourth period class too. Let's walk there together."

"Sure," was her quick reply. She turned to her lunch buddies, "See, you later, guys."

As they left the cafeteria, Josh explained, "You won't have to sit with those people tomorrow. You can sit with me at the athletes' table."

Gabby couldn't believe her ears. "Those people are my new friends. They were so nice to me especially since I'm the new girl."

"But I'm offering you a seat at the table with the most popular kids at school, the athletes and their girlfriends. Anyone at this school would kill to be part of our clique. Just be thankful the stars have aligned in

## Chapter Five

the heavens, and you have been deemed worthy of a seat at our table," Josh finished smugly.

"No thanks," was Gabby's curt reply.

Josh almost tripped over his own feet. "You gotta be kidding me. I'm handing you one of the best seats in the cafeteria, and you don't want it. You're turning down an invitation to join the in crowd here at Whittleton High. What's up with that?"

Gabby tried to explain. "I want to be friends with everybody."

Josh gave as exasperated snort. "What school did you come from? It doesn't work that way. It would be nice if it did, but it doesn't. There's only two choices. Either you're in with the cool, popular crowd, or you're a wannabe. Think it over before you decide. You can be dealt a lot of misery if you're on the wrong side of the social divide in this little kingdom. The athletes and their friends rule this campus. I'm not saying I necessarily agree with it being that way; I'm just telling you the facts. Let's talk about this later. Here we are at Mr. Derry's door."

Josh and Gabby entered the classroom and took desks next to each other. Josh felt so at ease with this new girl. It was weird, like there was some sort of invisible connection between the two of them. He had never felt this way before even with girls that were just his friends, and he had known for most of his life. But he was worried. What if she didn't come around about being part of his socially elite group? Could she be serious about being friends with everybody?

Was that even possible? He settled back in his desk. History was one of the few classes he actually liked in school. Mr. Derry was a pretty cool teacher, a walking encyclopedia of interesting facts. He also had loads of personal stories about his family and his travels that he shared with his students.

It didn't take long for the hour to pass. Mr. Derry ended the class with a homework assignment, read the first chapter in their history book. Josh groaned inwardly. He hated, no loathed, homework. It was the first day of school, and every teacher so far had given a homework assignment. What was wrong with that picture? Why did teachers burdened their students with hours of work to do at home? It wasn't fair. After a long day at school, followed by a long grinding practice on the football field, who wanted to go home and do homework?

Such was the life of a high school student. He should be used to it. Sports had been a part of his life as far back as he could remember. He had always been a big husky kid, so football was the natural choice for him to play. His dad couldn't have been happier. He had been a football standout himself back in the day.

As he gathered his books, he leaned over to talk to Gabby. "Think about what I said about sitting at my table tomorrow. Starting out on the right foot can make a big difference in your overall high school experience, and we all want to maximize that experience, don't we?"

Gabby sweetly smiled at him, "Alright, Josh. I'll sit at your table tomorrow, but I'm still determined to be friends with everyone. Deep down I think you would like that too. As a matter of fact, I think deep down you have a lot of things that you would like to do that

## Chapter Five

don't fit in with your snobby little group of friends who think they're better than everybody else just because they play sports."

Josh sucked in a deep breath. This new girl had just looked behind the carefully built wall he had worked so hard to construct to hide the feelings and emotions he didn't want anyone to see. What was it about this girl? His gut reaction was to try harder to hide his secrets from her, but he longed to be his true self with someone, someone he could trust.

So he asked, "Say, do you think you might want to watch me practice this afternoon. Some of the girls sit in the bleachers and wait for their boyfriends to take them home after practice. You can work on your homework while you wait. We practice about two hours. I know it's a long time to wait, and if you have something else to do, I'll understand."

Gabby put her hand on his arm. "No, I don't have anything else to do. I can wait. I'd like to watch you practice. I don't know much about football. Maybe I can pick up some understanding of the game while I wait. What position do you play?"

"Linebacker, someone as big as me always stands on the line. We protect the quarterback and crack some heads doing it. We really take some hard hits, but we give as hard as we get. We are going to have a winning season this year. Coach Barnes has worked us hard and expects a championship out of us. Football is pretty big in small towns around this area. On Friday nights, the stadiums are packed with screaming fans and proud parents. How come you don't know much about it? Where did you come from anyway? You never did say."

Gabby with a twinkle in her eyes remained vague with her answer. "I lived really far from here, and we had better things to do than play sports. I'll see you this afternoon."

She waved as she made her way down the hall to her next class.

Josh turned and nearly ran into his friend, Kyle.

"Hey, Joshie boy, why do you have that big dumb smile on your face?"

"Never you mind, my friend, you wouldn't understand if I tried to explain it to you."

"Ah, come on, Josh, you look like the fat cat who just ate the mouse," commented Kyle, who rubbed his friend's stomach in a circular motion.

"Get off me, you freak," laughed Josh, pushing his friend away from him in a playful gesture.

But Kyle came back with a more serious expression on his face. "Yeh, dude, you going to meet me at the usual place after practice for a little relaxation before you head home?"

"Not today, I got something else to do."

"Really, must be something pretty dang important to miss your date with Mary Jane."

"That's right, dude, it's something very important. I'll catch you later."

Josh left Kyle standing in the hallway with a puzzled look on his face. He continued walking down the hallway with anticipation building within him about seeing Gabby after practice. For the first time in a long time, Josh was looking forward to something that didn't involve smoking marijuana.

# CHAPTER SIX

Football practice dragged on for what seemed like forever that afternoon. Josh couldn't keep his mind on the plays, and Coach Barnes was furious with him, constantly yelling and waving his arms in a wild fashion that showed the coach's frustration. Periodically, Josh would sneak a peek in the bleachers to see Gabby sitting there watching him intently. It was strange, but it gave him a peacefully feeling on the inside to see her up there. But her presence was definitely a distraction. He took a direct hit from a fellow linebacker that sent him sprawling into the dirt. The force took the wind out of him for a second. The coach's wrath was swift and sure.

"Stewart, what's wrong with you today? Get your butt up now! Get your mind focused on the plays, or you'll be running up and down those bleachers until you drop. Understood?"

Josh tried to focus on holding his position. It was the linemen's job to protect the quarterback and give him plenty of time to throw the football or create a path for him to run with the ball. It felt really bad when he failed at that very important job during games especially those that ended up as losses. Even though he really wasn't sure why football games were so important, it weighed heavily on him if he failed to play his best. He knew he hadn't just failed himself but his team, his coach, parents, school, town, the list was endless.

Dimitrius Collins, one of the running backs, helped his teammate up. "Hey, Josh, don't let Sam hammer you into the dirt like that. Can't let him get away with that. Give as good as you get, bro."

Josh nodded at the advice, but before he had time to act on it, practice was over. They all dragged their tired, bruised bodies across the field into the locker room to shower and change. Later, a cleaned up Josh emerged looking in the bleachers to see if Gabby was still there. She was. He made his way over to her.

"Well, what did you think? I mean about the practice."

Gabby hesitated for an instant before saying, "It seems a bit brutal to me, all that physical contact, the hitting each other, just to move the ball down the field to score some points. But maybe I'm missing something."

"Yeh, like a stadium full of screaming fans all wanting their team to beat the living daylights out of the other team so their team can win. Winning is everything in sports."

"It's just a game, Josh."

"Try telling that to the crowd on Friday nights."

"Why do you play?" Gabby wanted to know. "Your heart wasn't in the practice like some of the other players; the intensity just wasn't there."

## Chapter Six

Josh was taken aback by the astuteness of her observation. She was right on. His heart wasn't in the game. He decided to answer her question truthfully. "I play because of my size. Look at me. I'm built like a linebacker. Everyone expects me to play that position. I started playing in the seventh grade, and every time I'd mention maybe I wouldn't go out for football at the beginning of a new school year, I'd see the crushed looks on my parents' faces. They love sitting right here in these bleachers every Friday night cheering for me and the team. Besides, everyone knows the football players are the coolest guys in the school. And everyone wants to be cool, right?"

Gabby looked deeply into his eyes. "Is that your ambition, Josh, to do whatever it takes to be cool, no matter what the cost?"

His answer was flippant. "Sure, why not?"

Gabby shrugged her shoulder, and Josh wanted to change the course of their conversation.

"Are your parents picking you up? Do you need a ride home?"

"No, I have my own car."

"Then I'll walk with you to the parking lot. My truck is there."

Gabby smiled and picked up her book bag.

Josh wanted to know, "Did you get any homework done while you were watching me practice?"

Gabby shook her head, "I'll do it tonight."

Josh grumbled, "Can you believe we have homework on our first day back at school."

There were lots of kids milling around the parking lot. Vehicles were packed with students anxious to get home after a long day of school and extracurricular activities.

Josh pointed at his red Ford Ranger with the fancy chrome hub caps. "That's my truck."

Gabby pointed and exclaimed with excitement. "That's my car." She was pointing to a pink Volkswagon convertible. "Isn't it awesome. I mean driving with the top down is the coolest thing ever. It's my second favorite way to travel. Flying is my first, of course." Her voice trailed off as she realized she was saying too much.

"I've never flown in an airplane before. I don't think I'd like it. I'm not fond of heights or tight spaces. This country boy hasn't traveled very far from home. Where all have you been?" He asked quizzically.

Gabby answered with a mysterious glint in her eyes. "I've been to some faraway places, Josh; maybe I'll tell you about them sometime but not this afternoon. It's getting late." She slung her book bag into the backseat, opened the door, and slide into the driver's seat.

Josh reached out and shut the door of the car, but he couldn't bear the thought of seeing his new friend drive away. He realized deep inside himself that this was a day like no other in his life. He had been waiting for that special someone, someone to give meaning to his life, who could help him sort out some things and give him focus and a reason for it all. And she had walked through the doors of the school that morning.

"Gabby, come home with me and meet my parents. I know it's the first day of school and all, but it'd be great if you could. My granny lives with us. She's the best. She's been sick lately though. I'd really like for

## Chapter Six

you to meet her because she means a lot to me." His voice quivered a little with that last bit of information. What was wrong with him? His insides felt like jello. He looked into Gabby's face and saw compassion there.

"Sure, I would like to meet your family, Josh."

"Great! Follow me. It's not too far."

Josh hurried to his truck and pulled out of the parking lot with Gabby behind him. The drive wasn't long. Whittleton was your typical small southern town with only a couple of red lights around the main square dotted with local businesses. Then the residential area spread out to encompass the one elementary school and high school, hospital, library, post office and such. There were the older homes built close to the town square, but Josh lived on the outskirts of town. His home was situated in a newer subdivision on an acre lot with plenty of room for a kid to roam and play. It had been a great place to grow up.

Josh's mind raced ahead of his vehicle. His parents would be so surprised that he had brought a girl home from school especially on the first day of school. At sixteen, Josh had never been serious about any girl. Oh, he had friends that were girls; they said he was a good listener. But this was different. While his parents' reaction to Gabby would be curious and cordial, Josh wanted his grandmother's approval very much. He bet his granny would see how special Gabby was the minute she laid eyes on her.

Mrs. Beatrice Adelaide Brewster Stewart had that unique quality. Granny Bea could sum up a person on first glance, see right to the core of a person. So much so, that often Josh had squirmed under the scrutiny of those piercing blue eyes. Granny could smell a lie as it came out of a person's mouth. Then she wouldn't be satisfied until she had uncovered the whole sinking mess that had made you lie in the first place. Josh had learned all about his granny's uncanny abilities at an early age, and he loved her for them. Now Granny Bea was old and sick, and Josh was afraid of losing her.

He pulled into the driveway of his home. Gabby pulled in directly behind him. His parents were already home from work. His mom would have started fixing dinner; his dad would be relaxing in his recliner watching the news on TV. He opened Gabby's door for her, and they walked across the open carport to the back door. Josh hesitated for a brief second to wipe his sweaty palms down his pants legs and give Gabby a nervous smile before he grabbed the door knob and entered the house.

His mother was standing at the kitchen sink washing lettuce for a salad. She started speaking when she heard the door open. "Hey, Joshie, how did the first day of school go?" She followed that question with another. "How did football practice go?" Her voice trailed off when she saw that her son was not alone. He had a girl with him.

"Hey, Mom, I'd like you to meet Gabby, a friend from school."

Gabby stepped forward with her hand out. "It's so nice to meet you, Mrs. Stewart."

Susan Stewart responded warmly trying to hide her surprise. "Same here, dear." She added, "Now I know most of the kids in Josh's class, so you must be new to our little town."

## Chapter Six

"That's right. It was her first day at a new school so I thought I would just make her feel welcome and show her around and invite her over." Josh's explanation sounded pretty lame, but how could he explain to his mother that he felt compelled to bring Gabby home with him and introduce her to his family, especially Granny. "How's Granny today?"

"About the same; she was napping when I looked in on her almost an hour ago."

Josh motioned for Gabby to follow him down the hallway. They stopped at the first door closest to the kitchen. He carefully opened the door and put his finger to his lips to let Gabby know they should be quiet. An elderly woman lay on the bed in the middle of the room. Her white hair was combed back to exposed a deeply wrinkled face. Her shallow breathing barely lifted her small frame that was covered by a powder blue comforter embroidered with white daisies. Josh and Gabby tiptoed to the foot of the bed.

Josh whispered to his new friend, "This is my Granny Bea, my dad's mother. Everyone in town calls her Miss Bea. She's eighty years old. She's been really sick lately, but I hope she lives a lot longer cause she's pretty special to me."

At the sound of her grandson's voice, the old woman let out a low groan and opened her eyes. "Joshie, that you?"

"Yes, Granny," he spoke softly as he sat down next to her on the bed. He took her hand into his, and she squeezed it firmly. Josh let out a sigh of relief. There was still strength in her frail body. "Granny, I brought someone to meet you, a friend from school."

He lifted his other hand and motioned for Gabby to stand near him.

Bea Stewart managed to hold her head up ever so slightly from her pillow. She fastened her blue eyes on the young girl that was standing by her bed. In the darkened room, she could see a faint glowing aura of light radiating from the girl. She blinked her eyes several times to focus as clearly as she could. She barely heard Josh speaking as he introduced the girl.

"Granny, this is Gabby."

He was interrupted by his granny's quivering voice. "Have you come to help my Joshie?" There was an uncomfortable silence. Gabby was absolutely sure that Miss Beatrice Adelaide Brewster Stewart knew exactly who she was and why she was here. Josh was just embarrassed by his grandmother's outburst.

"Granny, Gabby is new to Whittleton. Today was her first day of school. I invited her over to meet my family because she doesn't know many people yet."

Bea let her head sink back onto her pillow. Her frail voice asked, "Is that right child? I thought you might be the answer to my prayers for my Joshie. I've been praying and believing that God would send someone..." She didn't finish the sentence.

The effort of lifting her head and speaking just a little bit had completely exhausted her. Her mouth was dry, and she started to cough. She pointed to the empty glass on her night stand. Josh immediately grabbed the glass and went into the kitchen to fill it with water leaving Gabby standing next to the bed.

Miss Bea reached out her hand, and Gabby took it. The old woman pulled the girl closer and looked

## Chapter Six

deeply into her face. With a questioning look in her eyes, she wanted to know, "Child, who are you really, one sent by God? Tell me the truth now. I'll know if you lie to me."

Gabby had no intention of lying to Josh's grandmother. "Yes, Granny Bea, I have been sent from heaven to help Josh. But you must keep it a secret for now, just between the two of us. Will you do that?"

Bea nodded and whispered, "Thank you, dear Father, for your faithfulness."

Josh came back into the room and held the glass of water to his granny's lips while she took several small sips. She closed her eyes and drifted off into a light sleep.

Josh and Gabby went to find Josh's dad who was reclining in his easy chair watching the evening news. "Dad, I'd like you to meet a friend of mine."

"Gabby, my Dad."

"Dad, Gabby."

"Well, how do you do, little lady," Brent Stewart immediately stood to his feet and extended his hand to greet Josh's friend. He was use to Josh's friends, boys and girls, coming and going through his house. He and his wife had always kept an open door policy for the kids Josh ran with because they wanted to know them and their parents. But this pretty little thing was someone new, and Josh had brought her home on the first day of school. Josh's dad had a big grin on his face.

"Nice to meet you, Mr. Stewart," Gabby replied as her hand was buried in the firm grasp of his calloused hand.

That same hand came down hard on Josh's shoulder with this question. "How was practice, Josh? Learn any new plays? Is the team going to be rip roaring ready for your first game? The town's counting on you guys to give us a winning season, don't you know?"

"Yeah, I know Dad, believe me I know. But do we have to talk football right now?"

"Of course not, forgive my manners, Gabby. Did Josh say you were new to our little town?"

"That's right, Mr. Stewart, I just arrived in time to start the school year. I'm from out of state, but I'm looking forward to experiencing some of that southern hospitality that I've heard so much about."

"Well, we won't let you down cause Whittleton has about the friendliest people in this part of the state. Say, where did you say you were from?"

Before Gabby could answer, Josh's mother stuck her head in the room. "Dinner is just about ready, you guys. Gabby, we would love to have you stay and eat supper with us."

Josh and his dad both chorused, "Please Gabby, please stay."

Gabby smiled at their obvious sincerity but refused the invitation. "Thank you for wanting to include me at your family dinner table, but I really need to go, and Josh and I both have homework to do tonight."

Brent Stewart laughed, "Homework on the first day of school. Boy, those teachers are real slave drivers, aren't they? Not like back in the day when your mom and I kicked up our heels in school, right honey?"

## Chapter Six

"Oh, Brent, we had our share of homework," Susan reminisced. "We understand, Gabby dear, maybe next time."

"Yes, definitely next time," Gabby agreed.

"Let me walk you to your car, Gabby," Josh volunteered. They made their way to the door.

Josh's dad called after them. "Come back anytime, Gabby. Any friend of Josh's is always welcome here."

"Nice to meet you, dear. Hope to see you again soon," was his mother's farewell.

In the driveway, Josh shut the door on the pink Volkswagon after Gabby got in. "What a great family, Josh. You are truly blessed."

"Blessed? Do you really think so? Well, maybe. I guess so."

"Josh, you need to be more grateful for what you have, a nice house, caring parents, a praying grandmother. Not everyone is so fortunate."

Gabby was right, of course. Now he would have one more thing to add to his list of shortcomings, being ungrateful. He shrugged his shoulders and felt that weight get a little heavier. He waved as she pulled out of the driveway.

"See you tomorrow," he called after her as she drove away. As Josh headed inside, his thoughts ran back over the day. He inwardly groaned when he thought about the homework that awaited him, but all in all, this had been the best first day of school ever. And the reason why just drove out of his driveway and was on her way home. He couldn't wait for tomorrow.

# CHAPTER SEVEN

Josh was waiting for her in the parking lot the next morning. He was leaning nonchalantly against his truck trying not to look too obvious when Gabby drove up. He had never felt this way before about anybody. He was so drawn to this new girl. He knew deep down in the deepest recesses of his soul that she was the one. He had that fluttery feeling in his stomach watching her park her car. Her hair was pulled back in a ponytail tied with a blue ribbon the color of her eyes. She smiled and waved; he strode over to open her car door.

She was the first to speak. "Josh, I'm so glad you waited for me."

So much for not being obvious, Josh grinned and replied, "My pleasure, Gabby."

Just then the bell for first period rang. The students in the parking lot began moving along. As Gabby was getting her book bag from the back seat, she noticed Josh's attention diverted to the girl who was meandering around the cars in the parking lot like

## Chapter Seven

she hadn't heard the school bell. His body tensed as she headed in their direction.

Gabby looked closer at the young girl. She was slightly pudgy with bleached blonde hair. Lots of make-up hid her teenage complexion, but her eyes were big and brown with long lashes. She was dressed in tight-fitting jeans and a low- cut snug top. She smiled slightly when she saw Josh but kept on walking.

"Hi, Josh."

"Ugh, hi, Jenna."

And that was it; Josh let out a sigh of relief. He had dodged that bullet or maybe not because Gabby's next comment was, "Jenna, who?"

He stumbled over the answer. "Huh, just somebody you don't need to know about. Nobody decent would want to know a girl like her."

Gabby responded with a puzzled expression, "What are you talking about, Josh?"

Staring at his feet and feeling embarrassed, Josh tried to explain the best he could. "Look, I don't know how to say this any other way except come right out and say it. But you might as well be warned from the start. Jenna is the resident slut of the entire school. She has been giving it away to anybody who wanted it since she was in middle school. She's treated like the trash that she is so stay away from her."

Gabby's sharp intake of breath caused Josh to glance at her shocked face.

"I know, I know, it's disgusting. Just avoid her like she's got the plague or something, and you'll be fine."

Gabby's shocked expression turned to one of sadness. "Is that what you do, Josh?"

"Heck fire, yes! You can ruin your reputation in a heartbeat if you're seen hanging around her. She's used goods, and everybody knows it."

Gabby couldn't help but ask, "And this reputation you're guarding so carefully is really that important to you?"

"Well sure, around here what people think about you goes a long way. It's like that everywhere, I guess."

Gabby shook her head. "Not where I'm from." She saw Josh start to comment, so she grabbed his arm and said, "We'd better hurry, or we'll be late for class."

The morning flew by. Josh couldn't keep his mind on what was going on in his classes. He was thinking about Gabby and lunch. She didn't have the typical reaction to Jenna even after he had explained the situation. And what did that comment mean that reputation wasn't so important where she came from? He would save her a seat in the cafeteria and continue their conversation. He knew everybody would be talking about him and the new girl. Let'em. It was about time he had a real girlfriend. He had waited a long time for the right one to show up, and now she had. He felt slightly giddy as the hormones flooded through his sixteen year old body. About darn time! He couldn't wait for lunch, and as if on cue, the bell rang.

As he made his way through the cafeteria line, he kept his eyes on the double doors watching for Gabby. The lunch ladies knew their students well, and he got extra helpings of his favorites. All the football team

*Chapter Seven*

got extra portions especially on game days. He paid for his tray and then made his way to his familiar place at the tables reserved for all the football players and their main squeezes.

Skip and Mandy were holding court as usual. "Stewart, my man, what's this I hear about you and the new chick?" A chorus of chuckles and a crude remark or two were tossed around.

"Can't wait to meet the girl who snagged you, Josh, and on the first day of school. She must really have some powerful stuff to get you interested." Mandy huffed in disbelief.

Josh bristled at her remark. "Well, you'll get your chance because there she is coming through the door. He made eye contact with Gabby immediately, waved, and pointed to the chair next to his. She smiled that sweet smile that was also reflected in her eyes. Her face almost glowed with a soft light. For the first time Josh actually noticed the cute dimple on the right side of her face. He got that fluttery feeling in his stomach.

She made her way to his table. He made the introductions. "Everybody this is Gabby, and Gabby this is Skip, Mandy, Doug, Amber, Gabe, Susette, Dimitrius, Charles, Xavier."

A flurry of hellos went round the table. The girls were sizing up the competition, but Mandy was the first to express her thoughts out loud. "What a lucky girl you are, Gabby, to catch the eye of one of Whittleton's Wildcats on the first day of school. Not too many people get the chance to mix with our clique as soon as they walk on campus."

"Damn straight, they don't. You got to earn your place on this team." Dimitrius mumbled with a mouth full of food.

"Lighten up, guys," Josh chided. He pulled the chair out for Gabby.

Just as she was about to sit down, she noticed the girl from the parking lot this morning saunter across the cafeteria. She was walking in a provocative manner that was garnering some attention from a few boys who were making crude comments, none of which seemed to phase her. She found an empty table in the back corner and settled down.

Gabby nudged Josh and said, "There's that girl from this morning. What did you say her name was? Jenna, wasn't it? I'd like to talk to her; let's sit at her table."

Before Josh could utter a word, Gabby walked over and sat her tray across the table from Jenna Taylor, the slut of Whittleton High. There was a collective gasp of disbelief from the Wildcat group surrounding him. Josh flushed beet red and sat down in his chair; his appetite gone. The comments were flying, but he didn't hear them. Gabby motioned for him to come sit with her and Jenna. He shook his head and stayed where he was. Gabby smiled that sweet smile and turned her attention to the girl across the table.

"Hi, my name is Gabby, and yours is Jenna, right? Would it be alright if I ate lunch with you?"

"You got the wrong table. I know you're new here, but I bet Josh told you all about me."

## Chapter Seven

"He told me, but that doesn't stop me from wanting to be your friend, Jenna."

Jenna's eyes narrowed, "Friend, I ain't got no friends. Don't need any either. What I got is a bunch of guys hot after what I'll give em."

Gabby leaned forward and said softly, "But Jenna, if you keep giving little pieces of yourself away, there won't be anything left for you."

"That's ok by me. Been like that all my life; I'm use to nothing left for me. My dad left when I was a baby. Guess he didn't have nothing for me. My mom has had a string of boyfriends in and out of our house, and the only attention they every paid me was when they wanted something, you know. Now I got a step-father who can't keep his hands to himself. Everybody wants something for nothing. That's the way my life has always been, and it ain't likely to change."

"You have to change, Jenna, before your life will change. You have a heavenly Father who loves you even if the men in your life haven't."

"Heavenly Father," Jenna pondered for a second, "are you talking about God?"

Gabby nodded enthusiastically, "Yes, of course, a Father who loves you and sent His Son to give His life for you."

"Hold on," Jenna put her hand up. "I don't even believe in this God stuff. My grandmother use to take me to church when I was little, and I'll admit those stories I heard were pretty interesting, but a real God up there who cares about me, I don't believe it. And by the way, did Josh tell you how he knows me?"

Gabby shook her head. "My grandmother use to live five houses down from his house. I use to stay with her when I was younger just to get away from everything that was going on at my house. I loved that old woman. And that church she would take me to was the same one Josh and his family attends. We use to hear those Bible stories together, Josh and me, but that was a long time ago."

Both girls looked across the room to see Josh pushing his food around on his tray. He was the only person in the cafeteria who wasn't staring at them. "When I would stay with my grandma, sometimes I'd walk down to Josh's house and sit on the front steps with him. He was a good listener, a nice guy, but like I said that was a long time ago. He and I are both different people now. He's the cool jock; I'm the school whore. Funny how things turn out, ain't it."

"I don't think it's funny at all. I don't believe for one minute that is who you really are or for that matter, who Josh is or wants to be. I want you both to see your true identity and the plans God has for you." Gabby spoke with heartfelt intensity.

Jenna Taylor let a tentative smile settle on her face. "I like you, Gabby. It took guts to come sit at my table. Maybe I do need a friend."

Gabby smiled back. "Maybe you've found one."

# CHAPTER EIGHT

The school day was over. Josh hadn't spoken to or looked in Gabby's direction during fourth period history class. He was still fuming from the humiliating cafeteria fiasco. Gabby seemed not to notice his pouting and participated in the class discussion about the native Indians and their struggles with the pioneers who settled America. Mr. Derry made some interesting comments about how some local landmarks and geographical features like rivers and such were given Indian names. But Josh heard none of it. He was counting down the minutes until school was over.

He was waiting for her in the parking lot. "We need to talk."

"Alright , Josh, what do you want to talk about?"

"Not here; take a ride with me. Can you?"

"Of course."

They got into Josh's truck and headed out of town.

"Where are we going?" Gabby was curious.

"Down by the creek, it's kinda a hangout place, you know, where all the kids congregate especially during the hot weather."

Gabby wanted to know. "Aren't you missing football practice?"

"Yeh, and Coach Barnes is going to be madder than hell."

"Well, what do you want to talk about that's so important?"

Josh looked at her in amazement. "You really don't know?"

"No I don't."

"Gabby, you embarrassed me in front of my friends, in the cafeteria today when you decided to sit with Jenna instead of with me. How could you do that to me?"

"But I asked you to go with me to sit with her, and you elected to stay with your teammates. What's the big deal?"

"The big deal is that you ate lunch with Jenna even after I explained to you about her reputation. Why would you do that? You saw the way she walked in and the way the guys reacted to her. It's because they know what she does. Probably half the guys in the cafeteria have had a turn with her."

"What about you, Josh, have you had a turn?" Gabby's face was very serious.

Josh turned a rosy pink shade. "No, no I haven't, but it's not because she didn't offer it to me."

"Jenna, is looking for love in all the wrong places. She didn't get her father's love, so she's desperate to love and be loved by anyone who will show her

## Chapter Eight

some attention, even the wrong kind. But God loves her. If she could just grab on to that concept, it would change her life."

"I believe in God, Gabby, but I don't think even He could straighten out Jenna's life."

"Don't say such things, Josh. With God nothing is impossible."

"If you say so."

"Of course, I say so. If only you or Jenna or anyone will just believe, God will do the rest."

"Ok, Ok."

Josh turned off the main road onto a dirt trail and maneuvered the truck down the embankment until they came to a stop near the creek. It was a fresh water source that fed a pond of mostly clear water that eventually developed into a small tributary that ran through the county.

"This is one of my favorite places. I've been coming here since I was little, and my dad before me. My grandfather probably came here too to cool off and have some fun with his friends. He died several years ago. Had a heart attack and died just like that." Josh snapped his fingers.

"Granny Bea owns a large piece of property not far from here, and when she dies, it will be mine." There was a sense of awe in Josh's voice at the prospect of inheriting the land one day. "The guys and *I come* here all the time especially during the summer and after football practice. We've had some good times here." He reached under the dash and brought out a plastic bag which contained several rolled joints and a cigarette lighter. He glanced over at Gabby to see her reaction. He could see no condemnation in her blue eyes, thank God, because he really needed a smoke. "Let's go sit near the water and relax," was his suggestion.

"OK, Josh."

They settled down in the soft grass at the edge of the stream. Josh fished out a joint and used the lighter he kept in the bag to light up. He took a long drag, held it in his lungs for as long as he could, then exhaled. Immediately, he had that familiar feeling of well-being spread throughout his body. He could feel the tenseness seeping out of his pores as he took another drag and blew the smoke out toward the water. In his hurry to get the effects of the marijuana circulating throughout his body, he almost forgot the girl sitting next to him. He took one more drag and offered the joint to Gabby.

She shook her head. "I don't need that, Josh, and neither do you."

On the defensive, Josh shot back, "Hellsbells, I don't need it. This is what helps me make it through the day. Just knowing that I can come out here, smoke a little dope, and feel like I don't have a care in the world is priceless."

"Really, Josh," Gabby sounded unconvinced, "is that why you mentally beat yourself up on the way home after the high is over. When that weight comes crashing down on you because you know how disappointed everyone would be if they knew your little secret. And I just imagine you might be disappointed in yourself, way down deep."

## Chapter Eight

"Hey, enough of the amateur psych evaluation," Josh joked nervously as he took another drag on the joint.

"When did you start smoking pot, Josh?" Gabby wanted to know.

"Back during the summer. And it's not like I'm the only one who does it. Everybody smokes a little weed now and again."

"But you're not everybody, Josh. That's your problem isn't it? You try to fit in, be like everybody else, but you're not."

"I'm a football player. I'm in with the movers and shakers. Our little group sitting at those two tables in the cafeteria are the social elite of the school. All I have to do is snap my fingers and get anything I want just because I belong to that special little clique. Everybody else is a wannabe, a nobody." Josh's voice trailed off.

"Well, Mr. Mover and Shaker, why are you so upset that a nobody like me sat with a nobody like Jenna in the cafeteria today? I'm not a member of your snobby group of friends, and I don't want to be. And if you were honest, Josh, you don't like the limitations being put on you in order to be among the so called elite of the school. Be the unique individual God created you to be. What are you afraid of?"

Josh took his last drag and threw the butt end in the water. The new girl had hit a nerve, and he stood up. "We'd better get back."

He held out his hand to pull Gabby up. She took his hand in hers and a slight tingling sensation passed between them. Josh pulled Gabby to her feet, and for a brief moment they looked into each other's eyes. Josh got that fluttery feeling he had earlier, and Gabby pulled her hand from his. She turned and walked toward the truck. Josh reached down and retrieved his bag of dope.

As they were getting into the vehicle, Gabby asked, "Who's your supplier, Josh?"

He didn't really want to rat him out, but he wanted to tell Gabby the truth. He had been telling too many lies lately, maybe even lying to himself. He didn't use to be a liar. "Kyle." There he had said it. Yep, his best bud, fun-loving Kyle, his friend since elementary school days. He's the one who turned him on to marijuana. He's the one he slips the money to when he needs a new bag of weed.

Gabby shook her head in agreement as if she already knew the answer. "With friends like Kyle, who needs enemies. But you do have an enemy, Josh."

He opened the door for her to get into the truck and closed it after her, laughing at the idea. "Me, Mr. Nice Guy, who tries to please everybody, who could that possibly be?"

Gabby's facial expression was very serious as she leaned toward the open window and uttered, "The one who whispers in your ear."

How does she know about that? Josh wondered as he walked around the front of the truck. This new girl was certainly different from any other girl he had known before. He slipped in behind the wheel and hoped she would change the subject, which she did.

"Kyle's not on the football team. Why are you friends with him?" Gabby wanted to know.

## Chapter Eight

As he backed the truck around and started down the dirt road, Josh explained, "He use to play in middle school. He was pretty good too til he broke his leg in two places. Doctor said he couldn't play anymore. So the team lets him hang around the fringes of our clique. Plus he serves a useful purpose as our own special supplier of just about any drug of choice. Kyle's cool, always cracking jokes and being the class clown. The teachers don't like him much, but he could care less about them or school."

"Do his parents know he's a drug dealer?"

"Of course, they don't know. His parents are like all other parents, clueless!"

"That's not true, Josh."

"Yes, it is. Parents, even well meaning ones, are wrapped up in their own lives, working, trying to provide for their families, socializing, never dreaming their little darlings are up to no good. My parents would be devastated to find out I smoke marijuana. I never want to disappoint them, but I need what pot gives me, just a little mellowed time out in this messed up world we live in. You can understand that, can't you, Gabby? God can cut me a little slack, can't He?"

"Are you worried about what God thinks?"

"Sure I care, but He knows the pressure I'm feeling. He's not going to hold a joint or two every now and then against me, is He?"

Gabby was about to answer that question, but Josh interrupted her. Pointing his finger out of the truck window, he exclaimed, "Do you see that water tower over there? Every small town in these parts has one. See that ladder going up the side? Well, in this town it's the rite of passage for every boy my age to climb up and write his name on the side of the tower. That's been the tradition around here even since my dad was a boy. He did it himself when he was a teenager. Once your name has been spray painted up there for all to see, the city sends a maintenance crew and paints over it. Every boy in this town knows that he won't be a man in the eyes of the people who live here until they see his name written on the tower."

Gabby was amazed, "Sounds like a silly thing to do just to prove a point to someone."

"It's a guy thing, I guess. You know how we macho men like to do wild and crazy things."

"Well, this certainly fits into that category. Have you written your name up there?

Josh shook his head and had an embarrassed grin on his face when he answered, "Nope, I'm afraid of heights. Yes, you heard correctly. Big ol Josh Stewart, linebacker for the Whittleton Wildcats, would pee in his pants if he tried to climb up that ladder. Just a big woose, and the whole town will know it soon enough if I can't find a way to get my name on that tower."

"But that's ridiculous, Josh. Doing something foolish and dangerous doesn't make you a man."

"Not in your eyes maybe, but in Whittleton it does. Maybe one day I can smoke enough dope to not care how high it is up there. All I know is that my name has to be written on the water tower before senior graduation, or my name is as good as mud around these parts."

Gabby let out a loud sigh of exasperation. She really had her work cut out for her this time. And she

## Chapter Eight

had thought her last assignment was tough. Humans never failed to amaze her with their myriad problems and struggles. But God loves them so much, and she had been sent to help Josh, which is exactly what she intended to do. And maybe a tiny bit of help for Jenna too!

Josh pulled into the school parking lot. He was sorry the ride was over because he wanted to talk to Gabby forever. He felt as if he had always known her and could tell her his deepest and darkest thoughts, knowing in his heart that he could trust her with them. Before he could say anything else, she quickly exited the truck and slid into the front seat of her vehicle. All he could do was wave as she drove away.

He found himself thinking about tomorrow when he would see her again. Deep in the pit of his stomach that fluttery feeling of anticipation and excitement started to spread throughout his body quickening his heart rate, creating a buzz that rivaled a marijuana high. And then it slowly dawned on him. This is what being in love must feel like. It was true that he had only known Gabby for a few days, but he had never felt like this about any girl before.

He pulled out of the parking lot and headed home. He wanted to put his head out of the truck window and shout to the whole town, no the whole world. Joshua Stewart was in love for the first time in his life, and it felt great! He couldn't wait until tomorrow.

# Chapter Nine

The Stewart home was dark and quiet. It was just past midnight, and everyone in the house was asleep. Granny Bea had been dozing on and off as she usually did. She took little cat naps. Her shallow breathing made her chest rise and fall in short bursts. As she awoke and her eyes began to adjust to the darkness, she noticed a faint glow from the corner of the room. Someone was seated there in the chair. "Who's there?" Her voice was faint but firm.

"It's me, Granny Bea. Gabby"

"Come closer, child, so I can see you."

Gabby moved the chair next to the bed, sat in it, and reached out and took the elderly woman's hand in hers. Immediately, the life force that glowed in the young angel began to transfer into Granny Bea. The woman let out a shocked gasp when she felt the warm energizing surge of power flow through her frail body.

Her eyes twinkled as she smiled at Gabby and declared, "I feel good enough to dance the night away. If Albert was here right now, we'd show you a thing or two about dancing, young lady. We could do it all,

## Chapter Nine

the fox trot, two- step, but the waltz was our favorite. That man could twirl me all over the dance floor, and I would beg for more. We made quite a pair, you know, back in the old days. But this isn't about the old days, is it, Gabby?"

"No, mam, it's about Josh."

Bea nodded her head. "Been praying for that boy for a while. He was the sweetest little boy." She stopped as she remembered her grandson when he was young. "But something has changed, Gabby, and not for the better. My Joshie is not the same sweet, innocent little boy any more. I don't know, he seems to be going in two different directions, and it's got him confused. I hate to see him struggle so. It's hard growing up nowadays. It used to be easier when Albert and I were young. Things were simpler back then. Even when we were raising our two boys, we had a pretty easy time of it. But times are different now; there's too much evil in the world." She stopped to take a deep breath. "Listen at me just going on." Granny Bea looked squarely at Gabby. "How are you going to help him, dear?"

"I'm not sure yet," Gabby answered truthfully. "But don't worry, I'll figure it all out before long."

"That's good because I don't have much longer, do I?"

"No, Granny Bea, you'll be going home soon."

She let out a sigh of relief. "I'm ready, and that's a fact. Ready to see my sweet Albert again, and my Donnie. Donnie was Brent's older brother, my first born. He died in a car wreck when he was sixteen, same age as Josh is now. They're waiting for me in heaven, and I'm anxious to go, but not before my Joshie is ok. Promise me that, Gabby." The old woman's grip on the girl's hand was surprisingly strong.

Gabby smiled and the dimple on her right cheek was showing. She readily agreed. "I promise."

Bea let out a sigh of contentment. She patted Gabby's hand with hers. "I know you will, dear. Could you spare a few minutes while I take a trip down memory lane?"

The glowing angel nodded her head and gave the elderly woman a smile of encouragement.

"My Albert was a good man, a hard-working man. We were in school together. That's where we danced for the first time. We loved to dance, Gabby. Al, everyone called him Al, would come home humming a tune, grab me into his arms, and twirl me around the kitchen. Sometimes we would move the furniture in the living room, turn on the radio, and dance the evening away. I loved that man. I miss him." Her voice quivered.

Gabby replied softly, "I'm sure you do. It sounds like a match made in heaven."

"Yes, dear, I believe it was. We were a God-fearing family, Gabby. We brought our family up in the church, taught them to love God, and live right. We worked hard, enjoyed ourselves now and again, but we looked to God as our source. Al inherited the property a few miles out of town from his dad. We built our house on it, raised our family there, and God surely blessed us. Al loved the land, had a deep connection to it. He had to work in a paper mill on the Gulf Coast to support us, drove almost an hour to and

## Chapter Nine

from work every day. When he got home each day, he would walk the land, checking on the livestock, or looking over the garden he had planted. And there was plenty for me to do, I guess, as a housewife and mother of two boys." Again her voice quivered.

Gabby leaned forward and said, "Tell me about Donnie."

"He was my oldest. Brent didn't come along until five years later. So Al and I had all that time to dote on him, and he knew it. Sweet boy though, loved the land just like his father. He could be rough and tumble like boys can be, but Donnie had a sensitive side. Talented too, he played the guitar, taught himself how to play. He sang in church all the time, had a voice like an angel." Bea glanced at Gabby. "Do you sing, dear?"

"The inhabitants of heaven sing praises to God on His throne continually. It's our great honor to do so. I'm sure Donnie is lifting up his voice in that heavenly chorus. Tell me how he died?"

"He was driving back from a game on Friday night. He played football, same as Brent and Josh. Al and I had been to the game; Brent, who was ten at the time, was with us. We went to every game. We were already home getting ready for bed. Donnie had just gotten his driver's license that summer. Al had bought him a used truck; he was so proud of it. And on the way home that night, his truck veered off the road and hit a tree. He was killed on impact. It devastated us for sure. It took a long time to get over it, if you ever really do." Bea hesitated and a tear rolled down her cheek. "So sad, Gabby, so very sad, and such a waste of a life not lived. We don't know what happened.

Did he fall asleep? Did he swerve to avoid hitting an animal? That's one of the worst parts of the hurting, not knowing or understanding the why of it. Did you know that, Gabby? That pain of losing my Al and Donnie is always with me. Does God know that?"

Gabby opened her mouth to answer, but Granny Bea stopped her. "Don't answer that cause I intend to ask God personally when I see Him."

The young angel smiled showing her dimpled cheek. She would like to eavesdrop on that conversation.

Granny Bea changed the subject. "Josh is a lot like my Donnie. He loves the land. It wouldn't surprise me if he builds his own house out there one day and raises his kids when the right girl comes along. If we can just get him through these teenage years, he'll be alright. Brent sowed a few wild oats when he was young, but he straightened out especially after he met Susan. They're good parents, Gabby; they raised Josh in the church. He knows right from wrong. How come he's having such a hard time making the right choices?"

Gabby tried to explain. "Josh is letting other people influence him too much. He won't stand up and be himself. He's like a chameleon changing colors to blend in with whoever he's with or to meet the expectations of others. He's really struggling to embrace his God-given identity. He's letting the pressure of trying to please everybody cause him to suppress his emotions and make unwise choices. Some of his friends aren't the best either."

*Chapter Nine*

"Huh, you must be referring to that Kyle. Smart-allecky and disrespectful if you ask me. Someone needs to tan his hide."

"It's not just Kyle; it's lots of other influences that's making it hard for him to think clearly right now."

Granny Bea commented. "That might be true, but I know my Joshie. He is a sweet kid with a big heart. He has always been a big kid, but instead of using his size to bully, he has been a champion for the underdog. He's got lots of admirable characteristics. I'm proud of him."

"You're right Granny Bea. Josh is a good guy who's gotten off track, and it's my job to help him find his way back onto the right path. He's so blessed to have a praying grandmother. I wish all parents and grandparents realized how important prayer is."

"Me, too. Prayer has seen me through the good and bad times. I wouldn't have made it this far without my faith in God. I don't know how people get up in the morning when they don't believe in a divine Creator. Al and I used to pray together. We prayed for Brent, and now I pray for Josh. God is faithful and good!"

Gabby released Granny Bea's hand and stood up next to the bed. "Yes, He is!" She leaned down and kissed the old woman on the cheek. "Please keep my visit tonight our secret, and Granny Bea, can I ask a favor of you?"

"Why of course, child, anything."

"Do you know Jenna Taylor? She used to visit her grandmother a few houses down from here when she was younger. She's in Josh's class at school."

Bea thought for a second. "That must be my friend, Doris Hunt's little granddaughter. Doris died a few years ago. We went to the same church. I remember the little girl used to come stay with her a lot back then. She was a sweet thing. Use to come play with Josh"

"Yes, she's the one. Well, she's being pulled down a dark path and making some pretty poor choices. She could really use some of your prayers. Would you mind sending some her way?"

"I'd be more than happy to include her in my prayers, dear. Are you going to help her too?"

Gabby didn't hesitate. "Yes, Granny Bea, I'm going to help her, too!"

# CHAPTER TEN

The next morning brought thunderstorms across the area. The hallways at Whittleton were crammed with students who normally waited in the parking lot until the first bell. Teachers were standing on duty at their doors trying to watch the kids as they hung out at their lockers and mingled in groups to socialize before class. After getting his books, Josh made his way over to Gabby's locker. She had a ready smile for him. His stomach churned, and he had that slightly breathless feeling. Before he could speak to her, Darius, a fellow football player, slapped him on the back.

"Can you believe this downpour, bro? If it keeps up like this all day, Coach will for sure cancel practice. That sucks cause we need to have our game on for the game Friday night. It really sucks, man."

"Yeh, it really sucks," was Josh's reply.

As Darius moved on to voice his concerns with another ball player, Josh leaned over and whispered to Gabby. "Personally, I love when it rains hard enough to cancel practice. Coach Barnes is probably in the field house cursing the weather and bemoaning the fact he can't work us like dogs this afternoon. Say, want to take another ride with me this afternoon if I luck out and don't have football practice?"

"If it's back to the creek so you can smoke marijuana, no thanks."

That stung a bit, but he said, "It's back out that way, but I won't smoke if you don't want me too. I want to show you where Granny Bea lived before she came to live with us. It's where my dad grew up."

"In that case, I'd love to take a ride with you."

"Ok, it's a date if we don't have practice." That fluttery butterflies in his stomach feeling flooded over him. It was pouring down outside, football practice would most likely be canceled if it rained like this all day, and he had a date with this girl who had come to mean so much to him in a short period of time. Could this day possibly get any better?

Josh looked beyond Gabby and smiled. "Look here comes Kyle. Is he a smooth operator or what?"

Gabby turned to observe Kyle making his way down the hallway. He was high fiving all the football players, plying the girls with flattering compliments, and even stopping to talk with some of the teachers. He was a master manipulator. Just a few feet from where a teacher was standing, he palmed a small bag of dope into a student's hand and pocketed the money. The transaction was done in the open with no one the wiser.

"Teachers are as clueless as parents," Josh announced to Gabby.

"Do they not care what's going on right under their noses?" Gabby wanted to know.

## Chapter Ten

"It's not that exactly. They can't watch everybody all the time. Most teachers really care about the students, but they're overwhelmed with everything else they have to do. And they're looking for thugs and known troublemakers to be selling dope on campus, not kids like Kyle. He's flying well below their radar. That's why he's making a killing off us."

"Josh, my man, anything I can do for you today?" Kyle said with a smirk on his face. "Or maybe the little lady might be interested in a little something, maybe some Ecstasy or a Xanax or two? I'm your man, Gabby. I can fix you up with anything your little ol heart desires."

"Knock it off, Kyle." Josh was embarrassed at the suggestion.

"Hey, don't hate on me, friend. Just trying to keep everybody happy." He pulled a roll of money out of his pocket and waved it under his nose. "Ah, the sweet smell of cold hard cash. There's nothing like it." He was about to say something else, but someone farther down the hall called his name. He put his hand to his ear. "Hello, another customer; business is good, my friend, very good. I'll talk at you later."

As he made his way down the crowded hallway, Gabby made this statement. "Have you ever noticed that his face doesn't match his eyes?"

Josh looked at her with a questioning stare.

"Kyle's face is all smiles; his words are so smooth, but his eyes are dead."

"What are you saying?"

"I'm saying your best bud, Kyle, has dead eyes. It's what happens when you let yourself be seduced by the darkness."

"Come on, Gabby, you're being a little hard on Kyle, aren't you? If he weren't selling dope on campus, someone else would be doing it. Why shouldn't he be the one raking in all the dough? The guy is a real entrepreneur."

"Have you ever heard that the love of money is the root of all evil?"

"Sure I have. I've been in church my whole life. I know a lot about the Bible."

"Really, you could have fooled me." Gabby's tone was one of sarcasm.

Again Josh felt embarrassed by Gabby's dig. Why did he care so much what this girl thought? Maybe it was lame to profess to know the Bible in light of the way he was behaving. He started to defend himself but stopped short not knowing exactly what to say. She had given him something to think about.

Actually, the conflict inside him about what he believed and how he was living was something that had been weighing him down for awhile. He knew smoking pot compromised his faith. But faith in what was exactly the question he had been asking himself lately. Josh was smart enough to know his future depended on finding the answer to that question. And somewhere deep down inside his soul, Josh had a revelation that Gabby could help him find the answer. He also knew that when he figured it all out those voices whispering all that junk in his head would stop.

## Chapter Ten

The bell rang for first period. Josh walked with Gabby down the hall, silently praying that it would rain all day.

Lunch time found a steady rain falling outside. The gang was seated at their usual table. Josh had waited near the cafeteria door for Gabby hoping to steer her to a place next to him. The two of them went through the line together talking about their morning classes. After they paid for their trays, they moved to the center of the room.

"Gabby, there's plenty of room at my table."

"Sorry, Josh, but I'm looking for...Oh, there she is." She nodded her head in Jenna Taylor's direction. "I'm eating with Jenna. You're welcome to join us if you like."

She was off across the room leaving Josh to decide what he was going to do. He looked after her, then looked at the table with all his football buddies and their girlfriends. He started toward that table, but halfway there Joshua Stewart did something that had the whole cafeteria full of students staring. He turned and made his way to the table where Jenna and Gabby were sitting and sat down.

Gabby had a warm smile for him, her dimple showing. Jenna couldn't resist. "Well, well, the mighty Josh Stewart, linebacker for the Whittleton Wildcats, sitting at our table. The gods are smiling on us today, Gabby. To what do we owe this honor?"

"Knock it off, Jenna," Josh said in a tense voice. He was very aware that all the conversations in the cafeteria at that moment were probably about him.

"What will your snobby football friends think about you mixing with the likes of me? I wouldn't want your reputation dragged through the mud on account of little ol me," was her sarcastic remark.

Gabby intervened, "Jenna, be nice. Josh use to be your friend."

"Use to be is the operative word in that statement. Remember, Gabby, I don't have any friends."

"But that's not true, is it, Josh?" Gabby questioned.

Josh was paying particular attention to pushing the food around on his plate and didn't answer.

"Jenna, you told me yourself that you use to go over to Josh's when you would stay with your grandmother. That you two talked a lot."

"That was a long time ago, wasn't it, Joshie. You haven't wanted anything to do with me for a long time, isn't that right? What could I possibly have that you would be interested in?"

That last statement pushed Josh to his limit. He slammed his fist on the table and looked at Jenna with an angry face. He exclaimed in a loud voice. "You're damn right, Jenna Taylor. You don't have anything I'd want. You know why? Let me tell you. Because I don't want what every guy in this school has already had, YOU!"

With that, he pushed back his chair, grabbed his tray, and stomped across the cafeteria. He dumped his uneaten food in the garbage and exited the room in a huff. The entire cafeteria sat in stunned silence. Seldom did they see such outbursts during lunchtime and certainly never from Josh Stewart.

## Chapter Ten

The two girls sat there momentarily at a loss for words . Then Gabby quietly said, "Oh, Jenna, must you be so hard to get along with? It's like you're trying to push everyone away."

"I guess I deserved that. After all he did have enough guts to come sit at our table. But, Gabby, Josh didn't want to sit at this table because of me; it was you he wanted to sit by. I saw the way he looked at you; he's smitten."

Gabby shook her head. "You're wrong, Jenna; we're just friends. We've only known each other for a few days."

"Yeah, you're probably right. What do I know about love anyway, nothing. My own mother could care less about me. She has always put her men friends before me. Even when I would tell her about the touching and other stuff, she didn't want to hear it."

"I'm so sorry, Jenna."

"Well, don't be. I can take care of myself. And what I do is my business, nobody else's. Josh is entitled to his opinion, and so are you. I don't care what anybody thinks"

"That can't be true, Jenna. God loves you and wants so much better for you."

"God! My grandma Doris took me to church when I was little, and I heard all about God. I heard those stories about Noah, Moses, David and Goliath, and many more. But you know what I found out about God, Gabby? He's never around just like my real father."

"But Jenna, that's absolutely not true."

"Not true. Where was God when I was growing up? Did He know I was having to fight off every man who came into my house. Where was God when my grandma died when I needed her so much. Her house was the only safe place I ever had. After she died, I had to fend for myself. I found out that God is just some made up character in a book of interesting stories."

"Jenna, if you heard the stories then you know that Adam and Eve brought sin and death into the world when they chose to eat the fruit of the tree of knowledge, the one tree they were told not to touch. The evil one, Satan himself, deceived them into disobeying God, and he's been doing it to mankind ever since. Why do you and everybody else blame God when bad things happen? It is the enemy that comes to steal, kill, and destroy. God is love, and his light penetrates the darkness."

"Yeah, well, I haven't had any of that in my life. That light and love stuff sounds good, but it's just talk. If there really was a God up there, and He loved me, my life wouldn't be the miserable mess it is." Jenna's tone of voice echoed her pessimism.

The bell signaled lunch was over. The students put up their trays and headed for their afternoon classes. Gabby followed Jenna out of the cafeteria. Her thoughts were heavy. She still had a lot of work to do in a very short time. This assignment was turning out to be more complicated than she had thought. She remembered her excitement when she found out her assignment was a boy. God and Granny Bea were depending on her to pull Josh back onto the right path.

## Chapter Ten

And deciding to help Jenna was her own idea, but she knew God would be pleased. Her stellar record was at stake. She wasn't about to fail so she needed to concentrate on a plan of action.

Maybe she'd see a breakthrough this afternoon. Gabby gave a long sigh. How simple it would be if both Jenna and Josh could see that the God they learned about in church when they were children was real. That He loved them so much He sent His Son to die for them. That an angel had been sent from heaven to point them in the right direction, but it would be up to them how things turned out. The choice was theirs. It never ceased to amaze Gabby how blind humans seemed to the reality of the choices they made or how quickly they wanted to blame others for the circumstances related to those choices. So many times it was easier for them to play the blame game instead of seeing things for the way they really were. Difficult times, tragedies, hurts, disappointments, failures, and the like often pushed people away from God when all He wanted was for them to run to Him.

She had to straighten this out and quickly. If Josh and Jenna could see themselves the way God saw them, it would make all the difference. The young angel was thinking so intensely about what she needed to do that if anybody had been paying attention as they hurried to class, they would have seen the new girl radiating a faint glow.

# CHAPTER ELEVEN

It had rained all day, and a light rain was still falling when the bell to end school sounded. The football field would be a sloppy, muddy mess, and football practice had indeed been canceled. No doubt Coach Barnes and the football team would be bummed out, but not him. He was sitting in his truck waiting for Gabby. They had a date. Well, not really, a ride out to the old homestead probably didn't qualify as a real date, but he'd take whatever he could get. Students were coming out of the school doors and hurrying to their vehicles trying their best not to get too wet.

Then Josh spied her, and she took his breath away. She exited the building's double doors nonchalantly as if she didn't have a care in the world. As a matter of fact, when she got outside, she tilted her head to the skies and seemed to relish the rain falling on her up-turned face. She was smiling as she walked toward his truck with her dimple showing. Her smile made her face radiate with light. She was practically glowing in the middle of the dreary wet

## Chapter Eleven

school parking lot. And that beautiful, glowing creature was going to get in his truck.

Oh yeah, he had it bad. He was definitely in love with Gabby, and it felt wonderful. Should he tell her how he felt? He didn't know. He didn't want to mess things up. Maybe……

The truck door opened, and she swung her book bag onto the seat. "I love the rain, don't you?" she asked. She pushed her damp hair back from her glistening face.

"Yeah, especially if it gets football practice canceled," Josh agreed.

"Josh, instead of praying for rain, why don't you just stop playing football?"

"Let's not talk about it, Gabby. I can't wait for you to see Granny Bea's old house, or I should say what's left of it." He pulled out into the traffic and headed south. "It's a little farther down the road than the creek. Granny Bea owns quite a few acres out there. And one day they'll be mine." He glanced over to see if she was suitably impressed, but she seemed more interested in the scenery.

It didn't take them long to be out of town driving down the two lane highway. Gabby observed, "There're certainly lots of trees in this area. What kind are those?"

"Surely you've seen a pine tree before? The South is known for its pine trees. My Papa Al used to work at a paper mill. No telling how many trees have been cut down to feed that process over the years. But we have to have paper products, lumber, etc. I bet not one kid at school ever thinks about the paper they write on; I mean, you know, that it came from a tree."

The rain had finally stopped, and the sun was slowly peeking out from the clouds. They had only passed a few vehicles on the road. Josh thought about bringing up Jenna and lunch today, but he didn't want to ruin the afternoon. He wondered again if he should tell Gabby the way he felt about her, but he wasn't sure what to do. It seemed like he couldn't make a clear-headed decision lately.

"Josh, look!" Gabby exclaimed from the seat beside him. She was sitting on the edge of the seat looking out of the windshield and pointing. "A rainbow!"

He pulled the truck over on to the side of the road and craned his neck to see, and it was spectacular. A brightly colored rainbow hung in the sky before them. Josh opened his door and stood on the floorboard with his arms propped against the top of the truck door and the top of the cab for a better view. He motioned for Gabby to do the same. "You've got to see this." She eagerly followed his suggestion.

It was his turn to point. "Look it goes from one side of the road to the other." On the left side of the road, the rainbow arched into a groove of trees, but on the right side of the road the rainbow colors went all the way down to the ground in an open field. It was something Josh had never seen before, and it thrilled him to be seeing it with the girl he loved. Life was good! He jumped down and ran around to Gabby. He grabbed her by the hand and laughed. "Let's go see

## Chapter Eleven

if we can find the pot of gold that's supposed to be at the end of the rainbow."

He pulled her to the fence and climbed over first carefully avoiding the barbed wire at the top. Gabby followed, adeptly managing the climb including the barbed wire that Josh held down as she crossed over. Then holding hands they ran to where the rainbow touched the ground. They reached the place laughing and out of breath. They stood there in amazement encased in the colors of the rainbow. It was a surreal experience.

Josh pretended to look for his pot of gold and faked disappointment at not finding it. He jokingly said, "Another lie told to gullible kids debunked. There is no pot of gold at the end of a rainbow."

Gabby couldn't resist asking, "Why do humans attach such foolishness to something so beautiful created by God to remind them that all His promises are true?"

Josh replied somberly, "I think humans use their creativity to try to debunk God."

Gabby's expression was one of sadness. "And yet that very creativity comes from their Creator. Why do so many people insist on worshiping the things created by God instead of the Creator Himself?"

"There are no answers to those kinds of questions, Gabby, so let's not waste anymore time asking them. Look the rainbow's fading. Let's get back in the truck and head for Granny Bea's place before it gets dark.

As they were climbing back over the fence, Gabby's foot slipped, and she fell against the barbed wire strung across the top of the fence. Josh tried to catch her but actually just made it worse. She fell backwards, and her left shoulder came in contact with the sharp prongs. A ripping sound erupted as her blouse was torn, and the wire dug into her skin. She quickly regained her balance, but Josh knew what barbed wire could do.

"Gabby, are you alright?"

"Yes, I'm fine."

"Let me see your shoulder." He could see the torn blouse and knew a gash underneath was probably bleeding already. His first aid training from gym class was about to be put to the test.

"Really, Josh, I'm fine." She turned to show him her shoulder.

He lifted the flap of material to look at her skin, and there was nothing there. A fairly large tear was in her shirt, but the skin underneath wasn't touched. How'd that happen? Josh had been on the receiving end of barbed wire before. The stuff was wickedly sharp and could cut through just about anything especially skin. But Gabby didn't have a scratch on her. Lucky for her he thought but odd.

They continued the few miles to their destination. Josh pulled off the highway onto a dirt road. The winding gravel pathway of a few hundred feet led to an overgrown front yard that must have been quite charming at one time. Two large oak trees stood watch on either side of the cracked and chipped walkway that made its way to what was once a modest home now in shambles. The back half of the house had obviously been engulfed in a fire. The roof on that part had collapsed. The rest of the small house

## Chapter Eleven

was heavily damaged by smoke and the water used to fight the fire.

"Oh, Josh, what happened here?"

"The back of the house was struck by lightning. It was in the middle of the night. Granny Bea was still living here at the time. My dad had been trying to get her to come live with us, but she wasn't having none of that. Her health was frail even back then, but she wasn't leaving this place. Not until this happened."

"How long ago was it?"

"A little over a year. It broke her heart to leave this place. She hasn't been the same since. Well, you've seen her. Her health has gone down, down. I wish you could have seen her before, Gabby. Granny Bea loved to garden. She worked in the yard, and she also tended a small vegetable garden out back even after Papa Al died. My dad was always telling her to slow down and take it easy, but she didn't listen. She loved this place, and so did I. Growing up, I loved to visit out here. We'd come lots of times for Sunday dinner after church. There'd be the best food, and we'd sit around the big table in the dining room. Papa Al would say the blessing, and everybody would wait for me to shout amen before we'd dig in. Then after dinner, Granny Bea would be in the kitchen washing the dishes. My mom would be helping out too. And you know what I remember. Granny Bea would be singing, and my mom would be singing too or humming along."

"What would they be singing?" Gabby wanted to know.

"Mostly gospel stuff, old hymns from church. It's funny the things you remember from your childhood. I spent weeks at a time out here during the summer. Papa Al would let me ride the tractor with him. I loved that. Both of them would take me down to the creek to swim. I use to sit on the porch in the evening and listen to them talk about the old days, you know, when they were young. They really loved each other a lot. You could tell by the look in their eyes and the way they talked to each other. Even as a kid I knew. I would feel it.

Just sitting there on the porch with them, I could feel the love, the kind of love that reached out and included me in it. I guess that's why I loved coming out here so much."

"How blessed you are to have such a loving family. So many kids today don't have that, yet it was God's plan for all children to be raised and nurtured by loving parents and grandparents."

"Yeah, I guess I never thought of it as a blessing. But you're right. I know lots of kids at school who don't have what I've got, two parents and a grandmother who care about me."

Gabby added, "Who pray for you."

"Yeah, that too. How do you know they pray for me?"

She stuttered, "Well, I'm just assuming they do; that's the kind of thing Christian parents do, right."

"Sure, I guess they do. Hey, you want to hear something really weird. That night, the night the lightning struck, Granny Bea was asleep in her bedroom at the front of the house. She had no idea lightning had

## Chapter Eleven

started a fire in the kitchen. The back of the house was engulfed in flames, and smoke was rolling through the house. Granny said an angel came and woke her up and helped her get out of the house. I know it sounds crazy, but she swears that angel saved her life that night. A car on the highway saw the flames and called 911. The fire fighters found her standing by one of the big oak trees in the front yard when they got here. What do you think of that?"

Gabby's eyes sparkled, and her smiled was bright when she replied, "I absolutely believe it, Josh. Why don't you? Don't you believe in angels?"

"I know they're in the Bible, but I've never seen one."

Gabby's laughter sounded like chimes tinkling in the wind. "Do you think Granny Bea would make up a story like that? How else do you think that frail elderly woman managed to wake up, get out of bed, make her way through a house filled with thick smoke, and end up unharmed outside. Angels are real, Josh, very real. We, I mean, they exist to do the bidding of God, who sends them to help people all the time. And just because you have never seen one doesn't mean they don't exist or that you might not see one in the future."

"Ok, ok, enough with the angel stuff! I'm just grateful Granny Bea was rescued that night by whomever. I hope she lives a lot longer. She means a lot to me."

"Josh, Granny Bea is old and tired. You can see that, can't you? She's lived a long, full life here on the earth. She's lived well, and her reward is in Heaven. You wouldn't keep her from that, would you?"

"No, no, but it will be hard to let go." He waved his hand in a sweeping motion. "When she dies, all this will be mine. It's already written up in her will, has been for awhile. She and my dad had a long talk. She knew he didn't love this place like I do, and she didn't want him to sell it after she died. So they both agreed that it would be mine. One day I'll build my house in the same place as the old one. I'll raise my kids on this land. Course, I won't have kids to the right girl comes along...." He paused and glanced over at Gabby. To his delight, she was nodding her head as if she could see into the future.

That butterfly sensation started in the pit of his stomach. His palms got a little sweaty, but he reached over and grabbed her hand. "Let's go; the sun will be going down before long. I need to get you back to your car." He opened the truck door; she got in, and he chivalrously shut the door behind her. The ride back to school ended too soon for Josh. The only conversation on the way back was about how beautiful the sunset was. As she got out of the truck, Josh spontaneously said, "Gabby, I ugh, I want to ugh tell you something ugh ..." his voice broke.

"Yes, Josh, what is it?"

"I'll see you tomorrow." And with that, he headed home with the knowledge that his life had changed all because of a girl with blue eyes and a dimple in her cheek. A girl who made the world a little brighter every time she smiled.

# CHAPTER TWELVE

It was Friday, and there was a definite air of excitement at Whittleton High. Tonight was the first football game of the season. The football players swaggered down the hall wearing their jerseys while the cheerleaders were plastering the hallways with colorful signs made the night before. Students were talking smack about how the Whittleton boys would tear the other team to pieces. Josh was at his locker waiting for Gabby. Every time a teammate would pass, they'd slap him on the back or high five him with words of fierceness about the fate of the guys on the other team. This was exactly the kind of stuff that Josh hated about football, the hype. Why couldn't it be just good clean fun, and not life or death on the field? This nonsense would go on all day culminating in a pep rally that would whip the students into a frenzy before the big game.

He kept watching the door for Gabby. He loved the fact that she didn't take all this seriously. In fact, he loved her, and he was going to tell her that as soon as possible. He let out a sigh of relief when she walked through the hallway door and made her way toward him.

She gave him a quizzical smile and asked, "Is it always like this on game day?"

"Pretty much."

"Poor teachers, I bet there won't be much attention on their subject matter today."

"You're right about that. Teachers know that game days are a waste. They usually don't plan too much, just try to keep the lid on the kids until the big game tonight. Say, would you like to eat supper with my parents and come to the game with them, ugh, maybe sit with them during the game. I mean if you don't have other plans."

"I don't have other plans, Josh, and I'd love to eat with your family and sit with them during the game."

That put a smile on his face. "And Granny Bea's been asking about you. Make sure you go in and talk with her while you're there."

"Of course, I will."

"And Gabby, there's something I want to talked to you about, something very important. I won't be able to tonight because of the game and all but maybe tomorrow."

Just as he was finishing his sentence, Kyle came hollering down the hallway full of students chanting the school's fight song. Lots of kids joined in, and it was a relief when the bell for first period rang, and students started making their way to class. Kyle stopped next to Josh and Gabby.

He jabbed Josh with his elbow and slapped him on the back. "Josh, my main man, ready for the big

## Chapter Twelve

game." Before Josh could answer, Kyle pulled out a small notebook and pencil from his shirt pocket. "Want to lay down a few bucks on the outcome of tonight's game? The odds are looking good for a Whittleton win tonight."

Josh shook his head. "No thanks, you know I don't throw my money away like that. Don't you make enough cash getting everybody to bet on the sporting events at this school without taking mine?"

"Just thought I'd ask, bro. You never know when you might crack and bet the farm. See you later in the cafeteria."

Gabby looked puzzled and was going to ask what that was all about, but Josh held up his hand. "I'll explain later. We'd better get to class."

Later at lunch time in the cafeteria, the game day excitement continued to build. When Josh entered, he saw Gabby and Jenna already seated, and he got his tray of food and made straight for their table. He immediately got flack from his team mates. It was a game day tradition that all the players sat together and talked over strategies discussed all week in the locker room. Even Coach Barnes and his assistant coach were in the cafeteria eating with the players.

"Hey, Josh, get over here, man."

"Stewart, get your butt over here."

All of which he ignored as he sat down next to Gabby, who said, "Josh, it's ok if you need to sit with the team."

"I'm sitting right where I want to be. Geez, I'll be with those guys the rest of the day and most of the night."

"Won't you be going to your afternoon classes?"

"Nope, the team will spend the afternoon hanging out in the locker room, fooling around, going over plays, talking smack, listening to Coach Barnes pump us up about winning at all cost, giving it our all. You know the usual junk."

Jenna couldn't resist, "Yeah, we know, Joshie, the life of a jock is real tough, right?"

Josh started to say something but thought better of it. Instead, he pointed to Kyle, who had just entered the cafeteria. "Now that, ladies, is one more smooth operator." They watched as he went around to every table, joking with everyone, writing down something on his small note pad. They watched the slick way money was exchanged right under the nose of the teacher on cafeteria duty.

Gabby was curious. "You promised to tell me more about what Kyle is doing, Josh."

Before he could answer, Jenna spoke up, "That blood sucking leech is taking bets on tonight's game." The disgust in her voice was evident.

"Now, Jenna, don't be hating my friend for making a little money. Kyle is quite the young businessman." Josh couldn't help but defend his friend.

Jenna snapped back, "That's all he cares about, money. Look at him smiling and laughing like he's their best friend the whole time he's pocketing their money. Look at his face; he makes me sick."

Gabby took a long look into Jenna's face and pondered her reaction to Josh's friend, Kyle. "Actually, the Bible says that the love of money is the root of

## Chapter Twelve

all evil. There is no doubt that Kyle loves money a little too much."

Josh was on the defensive again. "Evil, you must be kidding me. Betting on sports is an American tradition that's been around forever. There is nothing wrong with a friendly wager between friends."

"Do you bet on the games, Josh?" Gabby wanted to know.

Josh was squirming in his seat. "Ugh, no, I don't."

Jenna jumped in, "Why not?"

"Well, I just don't that's all," he struggled to explain. "It's not because I think it's wrong or anything; it's just that it would put too much pressure on me if I thought money was riding on the way I played during the game." He looked at both girls to see if they were following what he was trying to say.

Jenna wasn't about to leave it at that. "Look at Kyle taking all that money. I'll bet you those kids are handing over their lunch money, and if Whittleton doesn't win tonight, some of them won't be eating lunch for awhile. How about it, Josh, don't you see anything wrong with that?"

He shook his head. " It's their money, and they can do whatever they want with it. But it's not something I want to participate in. What other people do is not my problem."

Gabby finally voiced her opinion. "I'm glad gambling doesn't sit well with you, Josh. You're listening to your inner voice, your God- given conscience, and it's telling you not to participate. I wish you would be as sensible about smoking marijuana."

Josh quickly looked around and shook his head. "Wheez, Gabby, don't say that out loud. Someone might hear you."

But Gabby continued, "So many people ignore that inner voice and make the wrong choices. God gave man free will. Adam and Eve chose to disobey God and eat from the Tree of Knowledge of Good and Evil in the Garden of Eden, and mankind has been paying the price for that choice ever since. Wrong choices often have far reaching consequences. But you're wrong about it not being your problem. Kyle is your friend."

"What does that mean? I can't control what Kyle does or doesn't do. I'm not his keeper."

Gabby replied, "No, but you are his friend. You could talk with him and try and make him see the harm he's doing to kids who need their money for lunch, not betting on football games."

Josh groaned, "You must be kidding. Do you really think me telling Kyle to stop taking bets on the games is going to stop him. No way!"

"But you could try," Gabby was insistent.

Jenna took Josh's side. "He'd be wasting his breath on that scum bag. You don't know how low he would stoop to make a buck. He's a parasite living off the misery of others." Her voice was full of hatred.

Gabby wanted to know the source of it. "Jenna, what are you talking about? What else is Kyle involved in?"

It was Jenna's turn to squirm in her seat. "Oh, how would I know. But if he's selling drugs and taking bets

## Chapter Twelve

on football games, who knows what else he's up to. Nothing would surprise me about him, nothing."

"You've got him all wrong, Jenna. Kyle's just Kyle. What can I say. The three of us were friends back when we were younger."

She picked up her tray and stood up. "Let me correct you. Kyle was never my friend. He was yours. Joshua Stewart, you amaze me. You're so naïve. You can't even smell evil when it's right under your nose." She wrinkled her own nose as if she smelled something disgusting. "Gabby, I'll see you tonight at the game."

They watched her leave the cafeteria. Josh shrugged his shoulders. "What was she talking about, smelling evil?"

Gabby replied, "I don't know, but I intend to find out."

"Gabby, don't get involved in Jenna's business. Girls like her, they can take care of themselves."

"Girls like her? What does that mean exactly, Josh?"

"I've already explained it to you. Jenna is kinda passed around from boy to boy at school. It's her reputation, her choice, I guess."

"Josh, sometimes you need to look beyond the choices to see the reasons for them. It is a bit shallow of you not to look any deeper than the surface. Everything is not always what it seems. A little discernment is a useful skill to have." She stood up. "I'll see you tonight after the game."

"My parents are expecting you around five o'clock. The game starts at seven. It's a Friday night ritual. I hope you enjoy spending time with my family and the game." Gabby nodded her head and smiled at him. She put her tray up and headed to her first afternoon class.

Josh sat at the table his excitement mounting, not because of the big game, but the fact that Gabby was going to be in the stands to watch him play. He glanced over to his team mates. He hoped he played well tonight. He put his tray up just as Coach Barnes ordered the team out of the cafeteria and down to the field house locker room to wait for the first game of the football season. The excitement and anticipation was building in the players. As he made his way to the football stadium with the rest of the team, his mind wasn't on football at all. Josh asked himself one question. "What the heck did discernment mean?"

# CHAPTER THIRTEEN

Gabby rang the doorbell of the Stewart home at five o'clock that afternoon. Josh's dad answered the door and cheerfully greeted her with a big bear hug. "Welcome, Gabby, welcome. Sue and I are so glad to include you in our Friday night football routine, a meal then on to the stadium. I can't wait. The first game is so exciting. It sets the pace for the whole season. You can really get a feel for how the team will play for the season, and I just know it's going to be a winning one for the boys."

Susan Stewart called from the kitchen, "Brent, don't bore her to death with football talk before she has a chance to eat supper. Come in here, dear."

Gabby followed the sound of her voice. Josh's mom was standing at the kitchen counter cutting up fresh vegetables for a green salad. Her smile was warm. "I hope you like spaghetti pie, Gabby. That's what's in the oven. It's one of Josh's favorites. It's too bad he won't be able to enjoy it with us tonight, but there will be plenty of leftovers for tomorrow."

Susan was looking at Gabby standing in the doorway. The young girl was dressed in blue jeans, with a simple pullover blue top, which matched the intense blue of her eyes. Her wavy brown hair was casually pulled back and held in place with a blue ribbon. Her face which wasn't caked in makeup as so many young girls wore today was soft with a warm smile. No pretense in this child, thank goodness. Josh had picked well. What a relief!

"Come in and sit at the kitchen table, Gabby. It'll be about thirty minutes before everything is on the table. Tell me about yourself."

Gabby didn't move from the doorway. "If you don't mind, Mrs. Stewart, I'd like to pop in and say hello to Granny Bea."

"How sweet of you. I'm sure she would love a visitor. Just go on down the hall. You remember where her room is from your last visit, don't you?"

"Yes, thank you."

Gabby made her way to the room. She gently knocked as she opened the door and stuck her head inside. "Granny Bea," she called softly. The old woman lay still on her bed with her head turned to the wall. Gabby called again, "Granny Bea."

Bea slowly turned her head. "Gabby, come in, child, come in."

Gabby questioned, "Did I wake you?"

"No, child, I was just thinking about the past as I often do nowadays. I think it's normal for someone at the end of his of her life to revisit the past, don't you? I have so many wonderful memories, good times and some bad too! But God has been faithful! His

## Chapter Thirteen

goodness and mercy have seen me through to the end. Come in and sit on the bed here next to me, child."

Gabby did exactly as she had been instructed, but her questions showed her concern. "How are you tonight?"

"Tired and ready to go home. I'm eighty years old, Gabby. I've lived a long, good life, but I have a home in heaven and loved ones waiting for me there." Her face took on a faint glow of anticipation. "Oh, to be with my Al again, and my son Donnie. And to see Jesus! I hope I don't have to wait much longer." Her voice strengthened ever so slightly as she continued, "You know I have been hanging on praying for my family, Brent, Susan, and especially Joshie. I've been worried about him for a little while. But now that you are here, I'm ready to go. I'm going home soon, aren't I? I can sense it. It's going to be soon, isn't it?"

Gabby reached over and took the woman's frail hand in hers; pulsating energy immediately was transferred between the two. She leaned over and spoke comfortingly to her. "Yes, Granny Bea, you are going home to heaven very soon."

"Thank you, God!" was her response. She squeezed the hand that held hers as tightly as she could. She felt strength surge through her body. "And Joshie, he's going to be alright, isn't he? I know God sent you here to help him. You are His answer to all my prayers I've been praying." Gabby shook her head to affirm what Granny Bea was saying. "You know, dear, I should have gone home about a year ago. There was a terrible fire at my home during the night."

Gabby interrupted, "I know, Josh took me out there yesterday. He really loves that place. He says it's going to be his one day.

Granny agreed, "Yes, he has the love for the land just like his grandpa. If Donnie hadn't died, it would have been his inheritance because he loved the land too. But it will be Josh, who carries on that legacy. Brent doesn't mind. He's proud to see Josh keep the land in the family."

Gabby made this comment. "I wish young people knew how important generational inheritance is. And I'm not just talking about land. Most kids today don't value anything or anyone old. It's such a shame because they're missing out on so much."

Granny Bea could only agree, "My generation's time is done, but there's a lot that can be learned from our mistakes. History will repeat itself if lessons aren't learned. But try telling that to someone Josh's age. I've tried to live a God-centered life as an example for my family, and I have spent many a night praying for them. I guess that's all one can do. Did Josh tell you an angel rescued me that night, the night of the fire?"

"Yes, he told me."

"Magnificent creature. I should have been afraid, but I wasn't. It all happened so fast. He woke me up out of a deep sleep. Thick smoke was already billowing through the house. I could hear the fire crackling in the kitchen in the back of the house. The angel gently picked me up in his arms as if I didn't weigh as much as a feather. And the next thing I knew, I was standing outside next to one of the large trees in my

## Chapter Thirteen

yard. It was raining that night; lightning was streaking across the sky. But my angel sheltered me under his huge wings until the fire truck appeared. Then he was gone. I sat in that truck and watched my house, the house that Al and I had built sixty years earlier, go up in flames. It was so painful to watch, and I didn't understand at first why God didn't take me home that night. But later after I came to live with Brent and Susan, I could see Josh was struggling. I knew I needed to pray for him, for my family, and that's what I've been doing. But, Gabby, I want to go home now."

Susan Stewart poked her head in the door at that moment. "Gabby, supper is on the table. Granny Bea, I have your tray right here."

"Susan, dear, do you think Brent could help me get to the table. I'd like to eat with the family tonight."

"That's wonderful. I'll get Brent. He'll be so surprised."

"Are you sure, Granny Bea? Are you strong enough?" Gabby wanted to know.

"After holding your hand, child, I feel stronger than I have felt in months. I want to enjoy my family in the few days I have left." She put her finger to her mouth. "Shhh, don't say anything about our conversation; death in never a pleasant topic to discuss."

Brent Stewart came in the room smiling from ear to ear. "What's this I hear? My favorite girl wants to eat with her family tonight. Mother, that is the best news I've heard lately." He threw the cover on the bed back and scooped up the fragile old lady in his arms. "Gabby, if you will get her shawl there on the chair, we'll go in for supper."

Susan had run ahead and made a place for her mother-in-law at the head of the table. Her son gently placed her in the chair, and Gabby put the shawl around her thin shoulders. Granny Bea glanced over the food and commented, "Spaghetti pie, Josh's favorite. Gabby, Susan is an excellent cook. I think you will like this as much as Josh does."

Her daughter-in-law was pleased with the praise, but she had to give credit where it was due. "If I am a good cook, it's thanks to you, and you know it. Gabby, my own mother died when I was a teenager. I didn't know anything about cooking when Brent and I got married. But Granny Bea took me under her wing and taught me a lot about cooking, cleaning, and a host of other things."

"And I loved every minute of it, dear. You were the daughter I never had, a welcome addition to our family."

"Hey, don't I get any credit? I'm the one who picked her out and brought her home."

"Yes, son, you did very well indeed. I only hope Josh does as well."

Everyone one at the table was smiling at the pleasant banter. It was Gabby who said, "It's a shame Josh isn't here to see and hear this."

Brent Stewart reminded everyone, "Joshua is right where he needs to be before the game, focusing on his job tonight. I'm sure Coach Barnes is going over plays and giving last minute instructions to the team. Playing well tonight is crucial if the Whittleton Wildcats want to dominate this season."

## Chapter Thirteen

Gabby asked an innocent question. "Crucial, dominate, why are those words associated with a ball game? I don't understand."

There was an uncomfortable silence at the table. Josh's dad tried to explain. "Well, ugh, Gabby, football is pretty important around these parts. Everyone will be at the stadium tonight, and everyone will be wanting a win."

"Why?"

Brent Stewart shifted in his chair. "Well, ugh, you see, ugh, spectators always want their team to play the best, be the best, well you know, WIN!"

"But I don't understand, Mr. Stewart, it's just a game. I don't understand at all why people care about unimportant things like games and don't care about the truly important things of life. It's a mystery to us." She stumbled to clarify herself. "I mean where I come from."

"Well, where do you come from, young lady? Because here in America, Friday night football is a big deal."

Granny Bea saved the day by interrupting. "The girl's just trying to say maybe it shouldn't be so big of a deal. I agree with her too. I was at every football game you played in, son, not because I enjoyed the game, but I was in the stands praying you wouldn't get hurt."

"Hurt! I was the one putting a hurting on the opposing team. And I loved every minute of it. Those were the good old days. Now I get to see my son do the same thing. It doesn't get any better than that."

Gabby said softly, "Good for you but not for Josh."

Brent Stewart looked long at the young girl across the table. "What does that mean?"

"Josh, doesn't like playing football, not the way you liked it when you where his age. He wouldn't play at all if he wasn't worried about disappointing you if he didn't." There it was. It had to be said. Gabby looked calmly back at Josh's dad.

"I don't believe it! Josh is a big ol boy, a natural for the game. Why wouldn't he want to play?"

His wife decided to answer that for her husband. "Because he is not consumed with winning, Brent, he's not like you. He has a softer side to him. He's not standing on that line thinking about whose head he can knock off on the next play. Josh has never had an aggressive personality even though he's always been a big kid. And there is nothing wrong with that."

Granny Bea chimed in, "Nothing at all! He was always the kind of kid to take up for anyone being picked on or bullied. And Brent, I'm telling you that Gabby is right about Josh. You've put a lot of pressure on that boy to perform well at something his heart's not in."

"I don't believe it. I've never pressured Josh to play football."

Susan Stewart corrected her husband. "No, you've just always assumed he would play and love the game like you did. He knows that, honey. He would never want to disappoint you."

"But he's never told me he doesn't want to play. My kid can tell me anything. I'd understand."

"Really, Brent, is that really the truth?" His wife wanted to know. "Because of the importance you

## Chapter Thirteen

place on the game, wouldn't your son's value go down in your eyes? Maybe Josh thinks so. I think it's time to re-evaluate what's more important to you, football or your son."

"You make it sound like I don't care about my son at all, and you know that's not true."

Gabby commented, "I know you love Josh, Mr. Stewart. But being a teenager can be a rough time, and Josh needs your support so he can be the unique person God created him to be. He's trying to figure it all out. But it's not easy. You remember what it was like when you were a teenager, don't you?"

"Well, sure I do, but I lived to play sports. I loved it; still do even though I'm just a spectator now. I guess I always just assumed Josh loved it too. But it's ok if he doesn't. I want him to be happy, to pursue his interests, whatever they are. I guess I need to have a serious talk with him about all of this."

The women at the table nodded their heads in agreement.

Susan Stewart spoke up, "Let's finish our meal and head over to the stadium. The stands fill up fairly quickly, and we want to get there in plenty of time to socialize with friends. Gabby, when you live in a small town, you know everyone, and they will all be at the game tonight. It's the biggest social event of the week, bigger than church on Sunday, I'm sorry to say. We would go even if Josh didn't play just to see everybody."

"But it's more exciting if your kid is on the field. And with a win, why, everyone will still be talking about the game at work Monday morning."

"There's nothing wrong with that, Mr. Stewart. Just don't limit Josh with your expectations. Let him know he has options based on what he wants to do, and he won't disappoint you if he's not on the field."

"Let the boy follow his own heart's desire, Brent. Give him the same freedom to choose just like your father and I gave you." This was Granny Bea's gentle reminder to her son.

He swooped her up in his arms with a light chuckle. "And I don't think I turned out too badly, did I, Mama?"

The old lady nestled her head on her son's shoulder and softly chided him, "I think you've turned out pretty well, my darling boy, pretty well indeed!"

"Now if you two young ladies will get this kitchen straightened up while I put this lovely lady back in her bed, we'll be off to the stadium."

As she watched her husband go down the hallway with his mother in his arms, Susan Stewart turned to Gabby and said, "Thank you, dear, what you said tonight at the dinner table needed to be said. Brent is a good man, and he loves his son very much. Don't think too harshly of him because he wants Josh to be a carbon copy of the athlete he once was. It's only natural for parents to want their children to follow in their footsteps. But both Brent and I want Josh to make the choices that are best for him. Making the right choices are so important, Gabby, you know that. Parents want their kids to have the freedom to choose, but they must choose wisely or suffer the consequences. We live in a dark world full of evil enticements, pitfalls, and danger. And I know peer

## Chapter Thirteen

pressure is pushing Josh in the wrong direction sometimes. I can only hope and pray that he makes more right choices than wrong ones during these teenage years, and that he comes out of them better because of the lessons he learns."

Just then her husband's voice came from the hallway. "Ladies, get a move on it. It's game night!"

# Chapter Fourteen

A little while later, the Stewarts and Gabby made their way across town to Wildcat Stadium. It was about six thirty, and lots of people were streaming in the parking lot. Some were standing in line at the concession booth, but many were making sure they found their usual seats in the bleachers. Gabby was following the Stewarts, who stopped and spoke to everyone they saw.

They finally started up the steps to the first tier of seats when Gabby happened to look down and saw Jenna and Kyle standing under the bleachers. She started to call out her name, but the look on Jenna's face stopped her. Gabby couldn't hear what they were saying, but she could see they were arguing. They were going at it pretty good. As Jenna turned and started to walk away, Kyle grabbed her arm and violently twisted it. Gabby would see the pain in Jenna's face. That's when she decided to yell her name and wave.

"Jenna, hey Jenna, want to come up here and sit with me?"

## Chapter Fourteen

The girl jerked her arm out of Kyle's vice-like grip and made her way from under the bleachers to where Gabby was standing.

"What was that all about? Did he hurt your arm?"

Jenna was rubbing her wrist. "I'm fine, Gabby. Don't worry about me. I can take care of myself. And don't worry about that scum bag, Kyle, either. He'll get what's coming to him one day."

"Won't you tell me what going on between you and him? I could help you if I knew more ..."

"No one can help me, and if the truth be told, I'm not even worth the effort of anybody trying."

"Oh, Jenna, don't talk like that. Look come sit with Josh's parents and me and watch the game. We can talk some more about whatever is going on with you."

"No, thanks, I've got things I have to do."

"What kind of things? Everyone is here to watch the game."

Jenna looked deeply into Gabby's eyes. "Not, everyone." The dejected girl turned and walked away. Her shoulders were slightly slumped over, and her head was down.

Gabby heard her name being called by the Stewarts, who were seated in their prime section of bleachers overlooking mid field. She smiled and waved at them, but before navigating to where they were seated, she took one last look at Jenna to see where she was going. To her amazement, she watched her friend walk to the entrance gate and meet up with Kyle again, the same Kyle who had twisted Jenna's arm so violently just a few minutes ago. What was going on between those two? She really needed to find out if she was going to help Jenna. She heard her name being called again. She maneuvered her way toward the Stewarts and sat in the place they had saved for her.

The cheerleaders were warming up the crowd with several cheers. The huge crowd for the home team and the visiting team was chanting back and forth across the football field. Then the home team burst onto the field with an ear-splitting roar of approval from the Whittleton side. Suited up in uniforms and wearing their helmets, it was hard to tell the identity of the individual players. Susan Stewart pointed Josh out for Gabby. He was wearing number seventy.

The team huddled around the coach near the sideline benches. The referees were in the middle of the field ready for the coin toss. One of the quarterbacks called the toss to see who would take possession of the ball. It went to the Wildcats, and the crowd went wild. Gabby couldn't believe the volume level of the thunderous noise. After all she thought, it's only a ball game. Humans never ceased to amaze her. Her attention was drawn to the field where the Wildcat offense had taken their places. Josh was on the line, and she could sense he was looking into the crowd trying to find her.

And indeed, Josh was doing exactly that. His eyes were scanning the section of the stands where his parents normally sat. His eyes were counting the bleacher rows right up from mid field. His parents liked to sit about mid way up. His dad swore that those seats afforded him the best view of everything that transpired during the game. He was still looking

## Chapter Fourteen

for Gabby when the ball was put into play by Skip Davis. Number seventy was quickly mowed down by an opposing linebacker. The breath was knocked out of his lungs as he hit the ground with this guy on top of him. The first play of the game, and he wasn't even paying attention. Josh groaned inwardly as he heard Coach Barnes yelling at him from the sidelines to wake up and play ball.

On the next snap he was ready, and he went toe to toe with his opponent. But he couldn't help but think how meaningless this physical exertion was when he could be spending time with Gabby. His eyes searched the bleachers again. Finally, he saw his dad, who was standing up, watching his son's every move with proud expectation written all over his face. Then Josh saw his mother seated next to his dad and next to her was Gabby. And again while he was looking away from the game being played right under his nose, he was slammed to the ground as the opposing team's players managed to sack the Wildcats' quarterback.

When Skip Davis hobbled up from the ground and huddled with his team mates, he angrily caught the face mask of Josh's helmet. "Hey, what is your freaking problem, man. Give me some coverage."

Josh mumbled, "I'm sorry." He chided himself about doing better. He could hear Coach Barnes yelling at him from the sidelines. He didn't have to see his dad's face to know that disappointment was there. He was letting his team down. Heck, he was letting the whole town of Whittleton down. He was a no good loser. Hadn't the voice in his head told him so many times before. He tried to shake off the defeated feeling that was overtaking his emotions. He thought about Gabby sitting in the bleachers watching him play. Her lovely thoughtful face seemed to radiate self-confidence, and her words were always encouraging. She made him feel good about himself when he was with her.

As the opposing team took possession of the ball, the offensive players came off the field as the defense took their place. Walking to the sidelines, Josh found Gabby again in the crowd. His eyes went straight to hers, and he immediately felt uplifted by the warmth and encouragement he saw. He knew without a doubt that she was on his side no matter what. He drew a sigh of relief.

Dimitrius, one of the running backs, interrupted his thoughts with a thump on his shoulder pads. "Hey Josh, Coach wants to see you. Man, where's your head at tonight cause it's sure ain't on the game, bro."

Josh steeled himself for the verbal lashing that Coach Barnes would give him. And he deserved it. Even though he wasn't all into football like the other members of the team, he had a job to do, and he needed to do it. He promised the coach he would get out there and give it all he had. And that's exactly what he did. The quarters passed quickly with few turnovers. At halftime the Wildcats were up seven points and managed to hang on to the lead to win the game by one touchdown.

Needless to say, the fans were jubilant and showed their enthusiastic support for the home team with waves of victory shouts and congratulations all around. Even Gabby couldn't help but be caught up

*Chapter Fourteen*

in the excitement of winning. She had a smile on her face that showed off the dimple in her right cheek. She also noticed the smug smile on Susan Stewart's face and the beaming smile on Brent Stewart's face as he slapped everyone near him on the back bragging about the team and the promising season they were going to have. Gabby wondered what it was all about really, this passion for a ball game. She looked at the home team walking off the field with helmets raised in victory and the visiting team leaving with heads bowed in defeat.

The more she contemplated it all, the smile left her face. There was definitely too much emphasis placed on this meaningless game when more important things needed attention. Oh, she didn't think having some fun was wrong; people needed an outlet for relaxation, a sense of community, and the friendly competition that sports afforded, but the serious issues of life didn't happen on the sports field. She thought about the individuals yelling and screaming in the stadium tonight for their team to win the game. What kind of situations were waiting for them at home? Gabby knew that God didn't care who won the game tonight. He cared about each person and the life he or she was going to live here on earth and the choices they would make. He cared enough to send an angel on assignment for anyone who asked for His help.

Susan Stewart motioned to Gabby, "Come, we're going down on the field." The whole home side was streaming out onto the field, congratulating everyone. They made their way through the throngs of people and found Josh.

His dad enthusiastically praised his performance. "Well Josh, you started a bit off your game, but you finally took care of business. Proud of you, son."

His mom gave him a warm hug. "So am I, Josh."

Josh turned to Gabby who was standing behind his mother. He desperately wanted her approval. Funny he thought. He had always wanted his parents' approval. Wasn't that the reason he was playing a game he cared nothing about. Wasn't the pressure of wanting everyone's approval: his parents, teachers, coaches, teammates, etc., pushing him into smoking marijuana. And now he wanted Gabby's approval above all else. What was wrong with him? Why was he always trying to be who someone else wanted him to be instead of just being himself. He looked into that smiling face and those twinkling eyes and saw exactly what he needed, not approval but acceptance. And dare he believe that those eyes held even more for him, maybe love. His heart leapt into his throat, and he couldn't speak.

Gabby commented, "You played well, Josh." She laughed, "At least, I think you did. I really don't know much about football, but your team won so congratulations." She leaned over and gave him a swift peck on his cheek.

His parents smiled sheepishly, and he fidgeted with his helmet. "Well, ugh, thanks," was his reply. They walked across the field headed for the locker room.

Brent Stewart spoke up, "Great game, Josh. We'll see you back at the house, maybe talk about some of those plays before we go to bed. What do you say?"

"Sure, Dad."

## Chapter Fourteen

"Gabby, Susan and I will take you back to our house so you can get your vehicle. We enjoyed you sitting with us during the game. We'll have to do it again."

Josh interrupted, "Ah, Dad, I'd like to drive Gabby back to the house after I shower and change clothes. Is that ok with you, Gabby? Would you mind waiting for me?"

"No, that's fine," was her reply.

His dad and mom smiled and made their way across the field to the parking lot.

"If you wait by my truck, it shouldn't take me too long to shower and change. I guess I smell pretty ripe right now."

Gabby, with her nose slightly crinkled up in agreement with his assessment, readily agreed to wait for him in the parking lot. She made her way through the thinning crowd, found Josh's truck, let the tailgate down, and sat there people watching. Everyone was in high spirits after the win. Parents were still talking about their expectations for this football season while trying to roundup kids who were running and laughing, not listening in the slightest to directives to get into various vehicles. Older students were milling about visiting with one group after another. Many were piling into vehicles and leaving the parking lot for home or going someplace to hang out until their set curfew. A few of them casually smiled or waved to Gabby. After all she had only been in school one whole week. She noticed one car pass through the parking lot with Jenna in the passenger seat. Gabby smiled and waved, but her friend didn't acknowledge her gesture.

It wasn't that long before she saw Josh coming toward her. By that time the parking lot was pretty much deserted except for the football players who were getting into their vehicles.

Josh crossed the parking lot feeling like his feet were a few inches off the pavement. He saw her perched on his tailgate with her legs swinging back and forth, that bright smile lighting up her whole face. He had never felt this way before, and it felt good; no it felt great. He felt like the luckiest guy in the world to have found someone like Gabby. He hoped he didn't do anything to mess it up.

"Ready to go?" He swung his backpack into the bed of the truck and helped her down. With the tailgate slammed shut, he opened the passenger door for her then got behind the wheel, and they were on their way. "What did you think of the game?"

Gabby worded her response carefully. "Definitely interesting, but truthfully, I don't understand the importance everyone attaches to it."

Josh put his head back with a snort of laughter. "Me either! Ugh, tomorrow is Saturday. Would you like to do something with me, maybe spend the day together? I thought we could ride down to the Gulf Coast and spend the day on the beach, have a picnic, talk. And when we come back later tomorrow night, Mandy is throwing a party for the football team to celebrate our win. We could go together, and it would be a good chance for you to get to know the right

## Chapter Fourteen

people, my friends, you know the football guys. What do you think?"

"Of course, I'll go. It all sounds very nice."

Josh glanced over thinking how many girls he knew who would be thrilled out of their minds to be invited to a football team party, yet Gabby just thought it sounded nice. Honestly, where did she come from? She wasn't like any other girl he knew. She really had no idea that after being on campus for one week, she had landed one of the biggest catches at Whittleton High School, Joshua Stewart himself. She was clueless, but maybe that's what drew him to her.

He was brought out of his thoughts when he pulled into his driveway. He quickly got out of the truck to hurry around to open the door for her. He had never been so chivalrous before, but now he couldn't do enough for this special girl. As she exited the truck, she was so close to him as he stood by the door.

Josh reached out and put his hand on her arm. He wanted to pull her to him and kiss that smiling mouth, but instead all he said was, "I'll see you tomorrow then. We'll leave here at nine o'clock. Dress for the beach. It will be hot. I'll get Mom to fix the picnic stuff."

He knew he had to let go of her arm. Gabby turned to go and said over her shoulder, "Looking forward to spending the day with you, Josh. See you tomorrow."

He watched her drive away. He swaggered into the house. On his way down the hall to his room, he peeked in on Granny Bea. Even though it was late, she was awake. She motioned for him to come in. He sat down gently on the side of her bed.

"Granny Bea, how do you know it when you find the one for you?"

The old woman's eyes twinkled. "The one what, Joshie, what have you found?"

"You know, THE ONE, the person you are supposed to be with, like you and Grandpa Al."

"Oh, so you think you've found that special person God made just for you, do you? And let me guess, you think that person is Gabby, even though you have only known her for a few days."

Josh corrected her. "It's been a whole week, Granny Bea, and I've never felt this way before about any girl, so that makes her the one, right?"

"Josh, honey, I can't tell you she's the one. No one can. That's between you and her and God."

"How did God get in this relationship?"

"Because He has the one picked out for you. It's His plan: loving someone, marriage, family. He came up with the whole idea, and His plans are always the best. Remember that boy, and you will live a long, happy life."

"Did God bring you and Grandpa together?"

"Sure did and saw us through good times and bad, same with your dad and mom. It's why this family is in church on Sundays. Say, you know all this, or have you been dozing during Pastor Tom's sermons?" She chuckled when she saw the guilty look cross the boy's face. She reached out and patted his leg. "Well, God will forgive you, but you need to pay more attention to what the pastor is saying, more importantly pay attention to what God is saying. He'll never let

## Chapter Fourteen

you down, Josh. He will show you the path to follow, listen to His voice, and trust Him."

The teenager nodded his head in agreement and bent down to kiss the old woman's forehead. "Goodnight, Granny Bea." He shut the door softly and made his way down the hall to his bedroom. He had a lot to think about but was too exhausted. He hoped to sort things out tomorrow when he shared his feeling with Gabby on their day at the beach. His head had barely hit the pillow, and he was sound asleep.

But back in Granny Bea's room, she was doing what she had been doing before she went to sleep for many years now, praying. She hadn't always understood the importance of covering her family with prayer. When she and Albert had been young and everything had been easy, she took things for granted. Then they were blessed with two healthy boys, and the years flew by. But when tragedy comes knocking on your door like when their Donnie died, you learn the importance of faith and prayer. When you are on your knees and hurting so bad you don't think you're going to make it, that's when you find God is waiting with open arms to listen as you pour out your heart to Him. It's the tough times that cement your relationship with a loving Creator. Granny Bea had learned that lesson many years ago. Looking back over her life, she had witnessed God's goodness and faithfulness over and over. And now, hadn't He sent Gabby to help Josh. She trusted Him to work everything out for her grandson's good. With that confidence, she closed her eyes and drifted off into a light sleep.

# Chapter Fifteen

Josh was putting the picnic basket and the quilt into his truck when Gabby drove up. He had barely been able to sleep last night because he had been rehearsing some of the important things he wanted to say to her today. She exited her vehicle in a crisp white buttoned down top and denim knee length shorts. A multi-colored belt tightened at the waist emphasized her slender frame. Her slightly curly brown hair was caught up in a pony tail with a blue ribbon neatly tied around it. She made him catch his breath which he slowly had to exhale. She never dressed in the provocative manner of lots of girls he knew. They liked to flaunt their stuff, but not Gabby. She looked so fresh and beautiful on this humid Saturday morning she positively glowed.

"You look as cool as a cucumber, Gabby." He groaned inwardly at the corny comment.

"Thanks, Josh, I guess that's a compliment around these parts." They both laughed.

"It's about a forty minute drive to the Coast, so let's get this day started."

## Chapter Fifteen

They were on their way, the picnic basket between them, with the windows down, and the wind blowing through the truck cab lightly caressing their skin. Josh had the radio on one of his favorite soft rock stations. He had left the CDs he normally listened to with his buddies at home. They were pretty much on the raunchy side, and he would have been embarrassed for Gabby to hear the crude suggestive lyrics. They didn't talk much on the drive. Both seemed to be enjoying the music, the scenery, and each other's company without a lot of conversation.

Josh was contemplating how different Gabby was from any other girl he knew. The girls at school talked incessantly about what amounted to unimportant drivel. They obsessed about boyfriends, their looks, and the latest gossip going around.

But not Gabby, and he felt so lucky to have found her. She had to feel the same way. Please, God, don't let this be a one- sided relationship. That was Josh's silent prayer. He was anxious to talk to Gabby and tell her how he felt. It didn't take much longer to reach their destination. He pointed down the main highway.

"Look, you can see the beach at the end of the road."

Sure enough when they got to the end of the main highway, there was the Gulf of Mexico. The white sand beckoned them. People were already out enjoying the beach and the water. Josh turned right onto Highway 90 which ran parallel to the water for miles. One small town after another merged into each other. All of them offered various amenities as they catered to tourists and locals who loved life at the beach. There were hotels and places to eat dotted along the way as well as several large casinos that offered a variety of accommodations for patrons.

Josh drove just a few miles before deciding to pull into one of the large parking areas that had restroom facilities close by. He and Gabby gathered up everything and made their way to a perfect spot not too far from the water. He spread out the patchwork quilt made by Granny Bea and plopped the picnic basket in the middle of it. He held out his hand, and she slipped hers into his.

"Let's take a walk before we settle down for lunch."

Gabby marveled at how shallow the water was as they walked along the shoreline. The tide was out, and they could actually walk on the sandy bottom which had been covered by the gulf waters just a few hours before. Josh explained to her about the barrier islands offshore that kept the high waves away and the water a dull gray color instead of the clear blue of other beaches like the Alabama and Florida coastlines. A steady breeze coming off the water felt refreshing as they meandered along with Josh pointing out things he thought Gabby might be interested in. She stooped to retrieve several sea shells, and Josh found a sand dollar for her as well.

They had probably walked a mile or more when they turned to retrace their steps carrying their sea treasures with them. They walked past a young couple with two small kids. The mom was sitting under a beach umbrella entertaining a toddler while the dad was tossing a brightly colored beach ball to a young boy.

## Chapter Fifteen

"I like kids, do you?" Josh thought the question was a good place to start.

"I love children, so innocent, so trusting, so precious." Gabby's reaction was promising.

So he added, "I'm planning on having a few myself someday, how about you?"

The young girl, hesitated for a brief moment, then said, "I won't be having any children, Josh."

"Well not now, of course, but someday when you find the right person. You know, when you get married and are ready. I mean way in the future." Josh was sputtering around trying to find the right thing to say.

Gabby shook her head. "No children for me, but I'll have lots to do to keep me busy."

They made it back to the quilt and picnic basket. Gabby sat down and carefully spread out her beach souvenirs, and Josh started laying out the sandwiches, snacks, and sweet tea his mom had packed for them. He was a little disappointed about her not wanting any kids, but he was determined to find out why.

"It sounds like you already know what you want to do with your life."

"Oh yes, Josh, I want to help as many people as I possibly can; it's my reason for existing. How about you? What are your plans?"

He thought about it briefly and was embarrassed to admit he didn't have any, certainly nothing as lofty and noble has wanting to help other people. There was a strained silence. "I guess I haven't figured it all out yet. I know some kids my age who know exactly what they want to do and how to get it, but I just kind of flounder around wondering which path I should take."

Gabby smiled and suggested, "Why don't you ask God to show you the path He has for you."

"God, how did He get into this conversation?"

"God created you in your mother's womb. He knows everything about you. He has a plan and purpose for your life. Ask Him to show you what it is, and He'll do it."

"Did He show you?"

Gabby nodded, "I was created to do His will."

The conversation was getting too deep, and Josh wanted to change the subject. However, what Gabby said struck a chord deep within him because he knew she was right. He needed some guidance from above. He had been trying not to let his relationship with God interfere with his relationship with his buddies. He wanted to go to church on Sunday, but he didn't want God involved with the rest of his week.

After all, as a teenager he just wanted to have some fun. But that decision had only brought about a war on the inside of him. Voices whispering to him, pulling him this way and that way, had caused him to make some poor choices. Confusion about who he was and what he wanted to do with his life had made him miserable enough to jerk the steering wheel of his truck toward a patch of pine trees. But everything changed the day Gabby walked through the doors of Whittleton High. He felt like he was being refocused onto what really mattered, and truthfully, God was a part of that.

He passed her a plate of food, and they ate, laughed, and talked mostly about school, the football game the night before, and Josh's memories of

## Chapter Fifteen

growing up an only child. Josh noticed that Gabby rarely shared anything about herself but was deft at drawing things out about him and his family.

After they finished eating and put the food away, they took the scraps of leftovers and walked down to the edge of the surf that had slowly started to roll upon the beach to feed the seagulls. The agile birds swooped and dived as the two tossed bits of food into the air. Before long, there was a large flock of hungry gulls squawking and aggressively dipping and diving for the tasty treats. When the last of the tidbits were tossed into the air, the birds weren't happy at all about the situation. They continued to make lots of noise and dive bomb the two teenagers. Josh grabbed Gabby by the hand and yelled, "Let's make a run for it."

They ran back up the beach to their quilt, kicking up sand, and laughing at their timely escape from the insistent birds. They flopped down and lay on their stomachs side by side facing the water. A strong breeze kept them cool and quite comfortable. Josh had his head propped up with one arm. He was looking at the girl next to him. Her one dimple was clearly visible on her sweet smiling face. Josh was thinking that the day was just about perfect. The only thing that would make this day any better was if he did exactly what he wanted to do. So he did it. He leaned over and kissed Gabby on the mouth. A long soft kiss on those smiling lips, and it was every bit as wonderful as he thought it would be.

"Josh," his name came out of those lips with a long sigh. Her face was flushed, and her eyes were wide.

He decided to jump right in, "Gabby, I know we've only known each other for a week, but you've turned my world upside down. I've never felt this way before. Call it love at first sight, call it anything you want to, but it's real. I want you to be my girlfriend. Gabby, I've been waiting for a girl like you. All the other guys on the team have steady girls; most of them are having sex already, but I wanted to wait, and boy, have they given me grief over that decision. They think I'm some kind of freak for not wanting to take advantage of what is so easily accessible. And you know what, sometimes I didn't even understand why, but I just knew I wanted to wait for someone special."

"Oh, Josh," was all that came from those lips a second time. He looked deeply into those blue eyes, and what he saw there was not what he expected. Instead of happiness and excitement at just being asked to be his girlfriend, there was a sadness in her eyes and a pained expression on her face. They both sat up cross-legged from each other.

He tried again. "Gabby, I love you. I promise not to rush you into anything. We can take everything slow and easy. But I want you to be my girl. I know you feel the same way I do; you've just got to. I know you're the one, the one I have been waiting for." He reached across and took her hand in his.

Gabby faced a dilemma she had never encountered before. She certainly didn't want to hurt Josh, but she knew he had to be told the truth. She put her other hand on top of his. "Josh, I do love you."

His heart leapt in his chest. He leaned over to kiss her again. He would never forget this day. But their

## Chapter Fifteen

lips never touched because Gabby added, "But not in the way you love me."

He sat up straight, a tenseness running through his body. "What does that mean?"

Gabby felt a tremendous responsibility to explain everything the best way possible. "I love you because God loves you, the way I love all of his created beings."

Josh's frustration spilled over. "There you go again bringing God into our conversation. What is up with you and God? And what does that even mean that you love me because God loves me?"

"God is love, Josh. He's a loving Father over all creation. He sent His Son so that humans could be in fellowship with Him."

"But what does that have to do with us?"

"I love you with the love of God, the love He extends to all who will accept it. It's not a romantic or physical kind of love. Please try and understand."

"But I don't understand at all. I know how I feel. I also know I have never felt this way before, and you're telling me I got it all wrong. That I waited for nothing. That I've screwed this up just like everything else in my life." Josh ran his hand through his hair, and his shoulders slumped. "Gosh, where's a joint when a guy needs one." He looked across the sand to his parked vehicle.

Gabby intervened. "Is that really the answer, Josh? Does smoking marijuana help solve your problems, or does it just make you not care about your problems?"

"What do you know about my problems, Gabby? You've only known me for a week. Am I such a loser that my many problems are so evident? And for your information, smoking pot mellows me out and takes my mind off all those problems for a while."

"But it doesn't stop the voices, does it? Those insistent voices that whisper in your ears, reminding you of your human failings, your shortcomings, the voices that suggest you're not good enough and tell you to end it all."

With a sharp intake of breath, he wanted to know, "How do you know about them? I've never told anybody about that."

"Josh, that night you wanted to shut the voices up so badly you actually thought about ramming your truck into a pine tree, what did you do when you came to your senses?"

"I...I asked God to help me because I couldn't deal with it anymore."

"Well, God heard your cry for help, and He sent me."

Perplexed he wasn't getting what she was trying to say. "Gabby, what are you talking about, that God sent you. What does that mean?"

"Your heavenly Father sent me here just for you. I came from heaven on assignment to help you, Josh, because you called on God, and He always hears and answers the prayers of people who acknowledge Him and ask for His help."

His confusion lingered. "Are you trying to tell me you're some kind of angel or something? This is crazy!"

"I'm not just any angel, Josh, I'm your angel, assigned specially to you. And I believe that's why you feel so connected to me on an emotionally level.

## Chapter Fifteen

You're calling it love, and it is. The bond between us runs deep, but it's not a romantic, sexual kind of love. It's more like I'm a long lost member of your family who's just been reunited with you, your parents, and Granny Bea."

"Do they know you're an angel?"

"Not your parents, but Granny Bea knew from the first time she saw me. She has been praying for you for quite awhile and knows I'm here to help you."

"How, Gabby, how are you going to help me? I'm a lost cause, a loser just like the voices tell me over and over. My whole life is a lie. My parents think I'm this obedient son, and it would break their heart to find out I smoke dope. I'm supposed to be this jock out on the football field, and I hate everything about the stupid game. All my friends think there's something wrong with me because I'm not having sex with every girl in school who's willing to do it. I sit in church on Sundays wishing I was somewhere else because I know God's gotta be disappointed in me. You've really got your work cut out for you with somebody as messed up as me."

Gabby smiled and reassured him. "Don't worry. I haven't failed an assignment yet, and you're my third one. God's has a plan and purpose for your life, Josh. I'm here to point you in the right direction. Then the choice is up to you. You're frustrated now because you can't figure things out. It's like stumbling around in the dark until someone hands you a light that makes the way clear. You are smoking marijuana because it temporarily dulls your senses, and your problems seem far away. But as soon as the buzz wears off, the problems are still there compounded with feelings of guilt that somehow you've let everyone down. Now guilt is really something the accuser can work with."

"The accuser? Who would that be?"

"The devil, of course. He uses everything he can get his hands on to condemn humans, make them miserable, drive them to do evil things, even commit suicide. It's his desire to sabotage the plans and purposes for God's children. And he has legions of evil ones to assist him. You're in a battle, Josh, between the forces of good and evil. It's time you realized you have an enemy who wants to steal every good thing from you, destroy your future, and kill you if he can."

"Well, he almost did the other night."

"But he didn't win, and you must be determined to fight him anytime he shows up. Be bold, Josh, stand on who you are as a child of God. Use the lessons you've learned in church on Sundays to defeat the evil one and the darkness he promotes. You shouldn't be embarrassed that you're waiting for the right girl to come along. How blessed you are for grandparents and parents who have modeled how a loving marriage is God's perfect plan. There is nothing wrong with wanting to do things God's way. After all, He knows best. The world doesn't think so. They greedily want their desires fulfilled now, denying themselves nothing, seeking after pleasure to fill the vacuum only God can fill. That's really your problem, Josh. You are in conflict because you're straddling the fence between good and evil. You want to fit into both worlds, but you can't. You sincerely want to do what's right, what will make your parents proud, yet you're

## Chapter Fifteen

allowing your friends, teammates, and your desire to fit in pull you into the darkness that surrounds them. You don't want to be labeled as a Christian because you think that's just not cool with your buddies. But life is all about the choices you make. Right now, you're not making the best ones. That's why I'm here, to hopefully point you in the right direction, to help you if you'll accept it."

Every point that Gabby made found its mark in his soul. He had been raised to recognize right from wrong, to live by a code of conduct that differed from the world, to stand up for what he believed, and not be ashamed of the gospel. But in his teenage years, he had pushed those beliefs aside in order to fit in with his friends, to be cooler, more popular. And all of it had left him deeply conflicted; so much so that he had turned to drugs as a means of escape even for a little while. What a mess he had made of things. He looked at the girl sitting across from him. His very own angel sent to help him; how amazing was that! He had known something was special about her the moment he laid eyes on that sweet face. And he was in love with her. How that was going to work out, he had no idea; but for now, he needed the help she so graciously offered.

He got to his feet and held out his hand to help her up. "We should head back. There's a party tonight at Mandy's. All the football team will be there. I'd like to go if you'll go with me."

"Of course, I'll go with you; a party is just the place to face down evil." Her confidence was evident,

But Josh inwardly groaned. What was he letting himself in for, he wondered.

They packed the picnic basket and folded the quilt, then trudged through the warm sand to Josh's pickup. He left the windows down so they could still enjoy the breeze and the smell of the ocean. The ride back to Whittleton took about an hour. Their conversation was minimal. Josh wanted to bombard her with questions about heaven and such but felt slightly foolish even believing that she really was an angel. He wanted to believe it, but it seemed so out there that he couldn't wrap his head around it. Certainly, no one else would believe it either. And Gabby didn't volunteer any more information about angels so Josh decided to change the subject. As they got to the outskirts of town, Josh drew her attention to the water tower that stood off in a clearing next to the road.

"See the tower. Every guy on the football team has climbed it to spray paint their initials on the side of it. Even my dad did it when he was in school. But not me, and you know why. I've already told you I'm afraid of heights. That's right, I'm a coward. The very thought of being up on that gangplank that circles the tower makes me want to vomit. I might look like a big tough guy, but I'm a woose through and through."

"You're too hard on yourself, Josh. Fear is real, but fear can be overcome with God's help. There is always going to be something in life to fear, but you must rise above it. If you don't, the devil will use it against you. Like right now, you're beating yourself up because there's something you think you can't do,

## Chapter Fifteen

and really who cares if your initials don't get up on the water tower."

"I do," was Josh's response under his breath.

They pulled into the driveway of his house at three o'clock. It had been quite a day, and he didn't want it to end. He suggested she stay and eat supper with the family. He knew his parents wouldn't mind. Gabby readily agreed and told Josh she had a change of clothes in her car for the party later. Both made their way into the house thinking about the day they had shared.

Josh was thinking that their special day had not turned out the way he had hoped after he had declared his love for Gabby. All that they had talked about still swirled around in his head. That angel stuff was down-right crazy, yet he couldn't imagine Gabby lying to him. He could only wonder how tonight might play out, but he had a feeling deep down in his gut that it would be a night that neither of them would ever forget.

# Chapter Sixteen

Brent and Susan Stewart were happy to have Gabby stay for supper. It was so good to see Josh with a close friend who was a girl. They were used to rowdy boys hanging out in their home, playing tag football in the backyard, or shooting hoops on the driveway. Their home had always been open to their son's friends, but a special girl, that was something new. Gabby was in the bathroom now freshening up from the day at the beach and getting ready for the party tonight. Josh was in with Granny Bea.

He was sitting on the side of the bed. "Granny, what would you do if you fell in love with someone who wasn't the one for you?"

The woman looked at the downcast face of her grandson. "Well, I'd be mighty disappointed, I guess. But I'd try to find some good out of the experience. Maybe this love that you feel is a practice run for the real thing coming later. You're only sixteen, Joshie, you have the rest of your life ahead of you."

"That's what grownups always say to kids."

## Chapter Sixteen

"That's because it's true. Do you think we weren't young once? That we had crushes and first loves before the right person came along."

Josh shrugged his shoulders. Honestly, it was hard for him to imagine the frail old woman lying in the bed as a young person.

"Listen to me, young man, instead of bemoaning the fact that Gabby is not the one, enjoy the friendship you have with her. Learn all you can from her; she's here to help you."

"So you know?"

"Know what?" asked the voice from the doorway. Gabby stood there dressed in a light blue sun dress, belted at the waist. Her wavy brown hair fell to just below her shoulders. Her eyes were sparkling, and the dimple on her right cheek was evident because of the broad smile on her face. She crossed the room and stood beside the bed.

"I know that you look lovely, dear. Doesn't she, Josh?"

He nodded in agreement.

"Did you have a good time at the beach, Gabby dear?"

"Yes, I enjoyed the outing very much. I even brought you something." She opened one of her hands to display several small sea shells. She placed them on the nightstand next to Granny Bea's bed.

"How thoughtful of you, dear. They remind me of the wonderful days I spent on the coast beaches with my boys and Al. Warm sunshine, sea breezes, fun times….all so long ago. I miss my Al and Donnie."

Her voice was wishful. "But I'll be going home soon, and we'll be together again."

Josh reached out his hand and placed it on top of his grandmother's. "Whoa, don't be in such a hurry. We still need you here with us. I need you."

Granny Bea gave him a weak smile. "I've done all I can do for my family. I'm worn out, and I'm ready to meet Jesus." She looked straight at Gabby as she made her next statement. "I can't wait to walk those streets of gold with Him and my Al. I bet heaven is better than anything I could ever imagine. What do you think, Gabby?"

"I think you are exactly right about that, Granny Bea." She leaned down to look into the old woman's eyes. "The human mind cannot fathom what God has prepared for those who love Him and have been faithful."

She sighed a deep moan of longing and said, "You two run along now. I'm tired and want to close my eyes and rest, maybe dream about being there. Have a nice time tonight. Don't be out too late."

Josh and Gabby both echoed together, "Yes, mam."

Granny Bea closed her eyes and turned her head but not before reminding the two as they closed the door to her room. "I'll be praying for both of you."

While Josh went to clean up and change clothes, Gabby spent time with his parents in the den. When he rejoined them, Gabby and his mom were sitting on the couch looking through a family picture album. His dad was reminiscing about Josh's childhood.

"I guess it's tough being an only child. All our time and attention have always been zeroed on him.

## Chapter Sixteen

We wanted to have more kids, but it didn't happen. I sure was glad I had a son to carry on our name. I've always been proud of Josh; he's a good kid." His dad's remarks made Josh cringe on the inside. How proud would he be of his pot smoking son? He knew the answer, and it made him feel miserable.

Susan Stewart got up from the couch and said to their dinner guest, "Gabby, would you like to help me with dinner. We're having stromboli. I made the dough earlier today. All we have to do is stuff it with meat and cheese and throw it in the oven. It's one of Brent and Josh's favorites. If you don't mind, you can help me with the homemade marinara as well."

"Of course, I'd love to help," was Gabby's gracious reply.

Later after the delicious meal, the family was back in the den watching TV. Brent Stewart asked about the couple's plans for the evening.

Josh was evasive with his answer. "Aw, we'll cruise around and see what other people are doing. I'm sure we'll all get together and do something. You know how it is, Dad, just hanging out with friends." He had no intention of telling his dad about the unchaperoned party at Mandy's house.

His dad laughed and agreed. "I guess there's not too much to do for young people here in a small town like Whittleton. There wasn't much to do back in my day either, but we managed to have fun and stay out of trouble. You know I trust you, son."

"Yeah, Dad, I know." He motioned to Gabby. "I guess it's time we headed out." To his parents he assured, "I'll be back before curfew." The two waved as they went out the back door.

As he opened the door of his truck for Gabby, he commented. "Parents, you gotta love them, but what they don't know can't hurt them, right? Keep them in the dark as much as possible. That's a teenager's biggest job."

"Really, what ever happened to honesty is the best policy? Nothing good comes out of deception. You're just setting yourself and your parents up for more hurt when the truth comes out. But that's a lesson you'll have to learn the hard way. And by the way, where are we going?" She had noticed the truck was headed out of town.

"You'll see." It wasn't long before he pulled onto the short dirt road that led to the water tower. He parked the truck and turned off the headlights. He reached behind the truck seat and pulled out a spray can of black paint.

"I think tonight's the night. Tonight is the night I face my fear." His voice was a little wispy just talking about it. His palms were sweaty, and he had a queasy feeling in the pit of his stomach.

Gabby wasn't impressed. "Josh, life is not overcoming fear so you can take some juvenile challenge to spray paint your initials on a water tower. Your fear is holding you back from being the person God called you to be. He wants you to stand up for what's right and not cave in to peer pressure. Those voices in your head, that's the battle between good and evil that's being waged for your soul. Which voice are you going to listen to? You have an enemy that wants

## Chapter Sixteen

you to compromise your beliefs, be just like the world, and who whispers condemnation to you every chance he gets. But you know deep down that you want the things God has for you, a blessed life with the one He has waiting for you. I know you thought it was me. But Josh, she is coming. Wait for her, and you are going to have a wonderful life. But you must start making better choices, choices that reflect the light not the darkness. God will help you. Just ask Him."

"You make it sound so easy. But it's not! "

"You're right, it's not. Nothing about living in this fallen world is easy. But you don't have to do it on your own. God is with you if you believe in Him and His Son."

Josh did believe; he had since he was a young boy. He gazed at the girl across the seat from him, and he sucked in his breath. Her beautiful face was alight with a faint glow as she spoke to him. His very own angel sent by God to help him. The truth she spoke penetrated his brain, and he realized how sorry he was for trying to keep this God he believed in contained to just Sunday church service. He was tired of the conflict that raged within him. He had let wanting to be accepted by his peers take him down a path he didn't really want to go. Being popular, hanging out with the guys on the team, trying to be cool had caused him to make some choices he wasn't proud of. But that was going to stop tonight. He was going to put an end to those voices that reminded him of his shortcomings. He put the spray can back behind the seat.

"Gabby, run your hand under the dash on your side and hand me my dope."

She looked surprised, but she did it. All she could do was point the way. It was his choice to take it.

Josh took the plastic bag which contained the rolled up joints and cigarette lighter in his hand. For a brief moment, he had this overwhelming sensation that he needed a drag on one of those joints more than he needed air in his lungs. And he knew that was the evil of it. He rolled down the window and sent the bag flying through the air into the night. With a sigh of relief, he faced Gabby with a wry smile on his face. She laughed out loud, and he joined her. It felt good, really good to make the right choice. He was going to make a habit of it.

"Well, what can we do? Going to Mandy's party is no longer an option. Got any ideas?"

Gabby had a surprise of her own. "Actually, Josh, I still want to go to the party. I want to check on Jenna. I think she needs my help."

"Well, sure if you want to. I'm sorry for the way I've been treating Jenna. I've been a jerk for sure, but I plan on changing my snobby ways. What kind of help does she need?"

"I'm not sure; we'll figure it out when we get there,"

Josh backed the truck up and onto the highway. It was just a few minutes ride to Mandy's house. It was a large two-story home at the end of a narrow driveway. There were other houses in the neighborhood, but several acres separated the well-groomed dwellings. Kids were everywhere, hanging out in the driveway, on the lawn, and inside the house. Loud music was blaring from parked cars, and it was evident most of the teenagers were drinking.

## Chapter Sixteen

Josh and Gabby made their way through the throng of kids into the house. Loud raucous laughter mixed with loud music greeted them. The whole football team was milling around with plastic cups in their hands. Selected girls who were deemed worthy enough clung to the guys on the team feeling so lucky to have been invited to such an exclusive party. Shouts of recognition followed Josh and Gabby as they made their way around the house looking for Jenna.

A slap on the back came from Darius. "Yo bro, bout time you showed up. Starting to think you wasn't going to make it. Your girl here looks fine, my man, real fine."

"Thanks, brother. Have you seen Jenna around?"

"Bro, what you want with that used piece of trash when you got this fine thing with you?"

They made their way outside to the pool area and found their host, Mandy sitting with her boyfriend Skip, by the beer keg that was supplying everyone with the alcoholic beverage they were consuming.

"Bro, glad you made it." Ship's speech was a tad slurred. "Damn good party. My babe here knows how to throw them."

Mandy chimed in, "Glad you brought the new chick, Josh. Break her in good now. Show her how we party here in Whittleton."

Josh flushed slightly at the suggestive comment. He looked over at Gabby who seemed oblivious to the party around her. She wanted to know one thing. "Mandy, have you seen Jenna? Is she here?"

"I'm sure the bitch is here somewhere. She's always hanging around the football team ready to supply them with everything they need, and I mean everything." She tilted back her head and snickered loudly. "But I supply you with what you need, don't I, baby?" She ran her hand up Skip's thigh in a possessive gesture.

Josh grabbed Gabby's hand and pulled her away from those two. "What's next?" he asked. "What if we can't find her?"

"She's here, I know it, and she needs our help. Just let me concentrate for a moment."

She closed her eyes and a strange calm came over her. Josh watched as a faint glow appeared on her skin. He was still holding her hand which was now slightly warm and tingly in his. He looked around to see if anyone was paying them any attention, and no one was, thank goodness because the aura surrounding her was getting brighter by the second. Suddenly, she pointed up to an upstairs window.

"That's where she is; let's go."

They moved quickly inside and made their way to the staircase only to find Kyle blocking their way. "Hey, you guys, where's the fire? What's your hurry? Josh, my best bro, you need some dope? This is your lucky night. I'm giving away samples of some new stuff here at the party. I give it away first; then they come begging for more. Genius marketing, don't you think?" Kyle reached into his pocket and pulled out a roll of cash. "You want it; I got it."

"I'm clean, man, and I'm going to stay that way."

The other boy scoffed, "Is that little confession for Gabby here cause I know better. That's what they all say til the urge hits em; then they come crawling back."

## Chapter Sixteen

"Forget you, bro, we want to know if you've seen Jenna?"

"Nope," was the quick reply, but his eyes shifted slightly to glance upstairs before he nonchalantly looked at them.

"He's lying," was Gabby's pointed assessment. She brushed by him on the stairs.

He reached out and grabbed her arm which was a mistake. He immediately let out a gasp of pain as if he had touched something red hot. "What the hell?"

Josh tried to follow her, but Kyle grabbed him by the arm. "Look, bro, I'm warning you. Take you girlfriend and get out of here. Don't come between me and my business."

Josh stopped and looked into his friend's dark menacing eyes as if seeing him for the first time. This was his best friend. He had known him his whole life. And the light of understanding finally dawned in Josh's brain. He put his hand around Kyle's neck and pushed him up against the wall. "You're pimping her, aren't you, Kyle? All the guys, they're paying you to use her. You sorry scum bag! The money from the dope, that wasn't enough for you, was it? Money, that's all you care about!"

"Damn straight! And I'm warning you, Josh, don't stick your self-righteous nose in my business, or you'll be sorry."

"The only thing I'm sorry about is having you for my friend." Josh disgustedly shoved Kyle away from the stairs and hurried up them to find Gabby.

She had located the right room. She whispered to Josh. "Jenna is in this room."

Josh tried to open the door. It was locked. He knocked loudly on it. Someone from inside the room yelled, "This is a private party, get lost."

Josh put his shoulder to the door and was about to break it down, but Gabby motioned for him to stand back. She stood by the door with her hand on the doorknob. That faint glow appeared to surround her again and was being transmitted to the doorknob in her hand. It began to glow as well. Josh watched in awe as she tried the door again; it swung open effortlessly. He and Gabby walked into the room. There on the bed was Jenna with a resigned look on her face. Four members of the football team were standing around the bed leaving no doubt to what was about to take place.

"What the hell! Get the hell out of here, Stewart! Can't you see this is a private party!"

Gabby spoke up boldly, "This party is over, guys." She walked closer to the bed. "Come on, Jenna; Josh and I will take you home."

One of the football players moved aggressively toward Gabby. "She ain't going nowhere. We paid good money for her, and we ain't finished our business."

Josh stepped closer to Gabby. "Listen, bros, you best go get your money back from Kyle, cause you're done here for tonight." He reached out his hand and helped Jenna, who seemed to be in a daze, off the bed. "Come on, let's get out of here."

The four boys moved to the doorway to block the three from leaving the room. One nudged the other and pointed to Gabby, whose glow was noticeable.

## Chapter Sixteen

Josh spoke up and reminded the players. "I'm sure Coach Barnes wouldn't be happy to hear about his boys being involved in such depraved dealings. So you, boys, just step aside and let us take this girl home."

Mentioning the coach was all it took for the boys to part like the Red Sea. They still grumbled, but they did nothing as the three exited the room and went down the stairs. In the midst of the drunken reverie, no one paid them any attention as they left the party. Kyle had mysteriously disappeared. Josh put the two girls in his truck and headed for Jenna's house.

Gabby was trying to comfort the dazed girl. "It's alright, Jenna. You never have to do anything like that again."

Jenna finally seemed to snap out of her stupor. "You, don't understand, Gabby. Kyle has pictures of me, embarrassing pictures I wouldn't want anybody to see. He'll show them to everybody if I don't do what he says."

Josh's hands tightened on the steering wheel. "Is that why you've been having sex with all the guys because Kyle was blackmailing you? How long has he had these pictures?"

Jenna put her head down. "Since we use to play together when we were younger when I stayed with my grandmother. He invited me home with him one afternoon, and his parents weren't there. This older boy was, and he forced me to do things I didn't want to do. He said he paid Kyle so he could do it. Kyle took pictures of me. I've been his slave ever since.

Doing whatever he said just so he wouldn't show those pictures around."

Jenna's confession turned Josh's stomach. "That sick bastard. Wait til I get my hands on him. He'll be sorry he was ever born."

His anger boiled over as he thought about his so called best friend, who he apparently never really knew at all. How could he have been duped so easily? Maybe needing Kyle as his marijuana supplier had blinded him to other nefarious things his friend was up to.

But things were about to change. He was going to walk through life with his eyes open, alert, and making better choices. That decision had been made earlier when he threw his dope away. There was no going back. He was going to be there for Jenna because she needed a friend. And he was going to turn in his football jersey and equipment Monday no matter what his dad might say. And he was going to wait for the right girl to come along. He was going to try his best to be the person God created him to be and follow the path that He had for him. And he owed it all to his heaven sent angel who had her arms wrapped tightly around Jenna, reassuring her that everything would be alright.

Gabby looked over Jenna's head, and her eyes met Josh's. "You're not going to do anything to Kyle. That would just make matters worse. But you can take Jenna to school Monday and stay with her while she tells her story to the school administration. They can call the police and have Kyle arrested and get Jenna the counseling she's going to need. I'll stay with her

## Chapter Sixteen

tonight, but promise me you'll take her to school on Monday."

"Of course, I take her, but where will you be?" As soon as he said it, he knew. This girl he loved and who had helped him find himself was leaving.

No…..his brain was screaming. Don't go, not now. He pulled into the driveway of Jenna's house. The two girls got out.

As they walked away, Josh called after them. "Gabby, will I see you before….you know….before…" He couldn't bring himself to say the words.

She smiled and waved. He hoped that meant yes. With a heavy heart, he backed the truck out of the driveway and headed home.

# CHAPTER SEVENTEEN

But he didn't go home. He had something to prove to himself.

Gabby sat with Jenna on the bed in her small bedroom. They talked in whispers so not to wake up Jenna's mom and step-father. There was plenty of time to involve them tomorrow. The traumatized girl was so ashamed. "How can I tell my story, Gabby? Who's going to believe me, the school slut?"

"Listen, don't worry about that. Once you open Kyle's can of worms, an investigation will uncover all that he's been up to. And Josh will be there beside you, backing up what you say."

"Do you really think Josh will turn on his best friend? And he'll have to fess up about his drug use. Is he going to do that?"

"Yes, Jenna, I think he will. Josh has been going down the wrong path, but thank God, he's seen the light. He wants to do what's right. He's always wanted to but couldn't find the courage to stand up for what he believes. That changed tonight. I hoped it changed for you too.

*Chapter Seventeen*

You don't have to be afraid of what people will think or say. You've been victimized, but you can rise above it. No one can stop you from moving forward with your life except you. Give yourself time to heal but don't stay the victim. God gave everyone the power to overcome evil and live a victorious life.. No one promised it would be easy, but it is available to those who never give up. Promise me you'll never give up, Jenna. God has a wonderful future for you. He really does."

"I do believe it. Somewhere in the core of me I know what you are saying is true. My grandmother Doris use to say the same thing to me when I was a little girl. Gabby, spend the night with me. Please! I need a friend right now. Go with me and Josh Monday morning. We're going to need you."

"If I could, I would. You know that, don't you? But my time here is over. I must go tonight. But you and Josh will be fine. It's time to stand up and be victorious over your circumstances. Never bow to evil, Jenna, choose the right path and follow it with all your heart.

And God will be right there with you, if you let Him, directing your steps and watching over you. Now try and get some rest tonight. Talk with your parents tomorrow and face Monday with your head held high. What has happened to you doesn't define who you are, my friend. The evil one will try his best to use guilt and shame to steal your destiny. You must fight for your future, and I promise you the possibilities are endless."

"But why do you have to go? Go where?" The confused girl clung to her friend.

Gabby smoothed the hair from Jenna's forehead and spoke softly. "I was heaven sent, and I must return. Heaven is my home."

Jenna's eyes grew huge. "I don't understand. What does that mean?"

"One day you will understand, and you will thank God for this moment in your life because it made all the difference. God is good and faithful, Jenna, never forget that. Let Him be the loving father you so desperately need in your life. He will never fail you. Now I must go. I have to say goodbye to Josh."

Jenna's heavy eyes closed just for a second, and her friend was gone. Oh, how she would miss her. She couldn't help but wonder about Josh's reaction to Gabby's leaving. She knew he loved her. She wanted to ponder more on the things her friend had told her specifically about heaven being Gabby's home. But the young girl had been through quite a lot tonight, and she drifted into a restless sleep.

It was late when Gabby stood in the Stewart's driveway. Josh's truck wasn't there. She knew exactly where to find him.

He had climbed the Whittleton water tower and spray-painted his initials on it in the rite of passage of so many teenagers before him. Now he was stuck on the narrow walkway that circled the huge tower for maintenance matters. He was shaking in fear; the adrenaline rush that had propelled him up the ladder earlier long gone. His fear of heights totally in control, and the voices inside his head were raging. Whispers

## Chapter Seventeen

were urging him to jump, end it all! Stupid to be in such a predicament, what a woose, on and on the voices whispered. His new-found resolve to stand up and be a person of excellence and courage was totally gone in the circumstance he found himself in. How was he going to get out of this fine mess? There was no way he was going to make it down that ladder. He held out his trembling hands. What was he going to do? He could already see the headline of the town's newspaper. WHITTLETON HIGH SCHOOL FOOTBALL PLAYER RESCUED FROM WATER TOWER WITH SOILED UNDERWEAR. He groaned inwardly and thought that maybe jumping was the answer. He closed his eyes and thought of the one person he needed now; he pictured her lovely face and soothing voice.

"I'm here, Josh."

His eyes flew open and to his utter amazement, there she was, standing on the catwalk near him.

He gasped, "Gabby, how did you get up here? How did you know where to find me? How?"

"It's not how, Joshua Stewart, it's why. Why are you up here, listening to dark voices again and contemplating jumping off this tower? You must talk back to those voices whispering in your ear. Tell them to shut up, go away, you're not listening to them. Be proactive; don't let them back you into a corner where you think there is no way out. There is always a solution to every problem. You just have to find it. God has not given you a spirit of fear, but courage and a mind to solve any situation you find yourself in, so stand up."

Incredulously, Josh stared at her. "My legs are shaking, and I'm afraid I'll fall."

Gabby inched closer to him. "First of all, take a few deep breaths and don't look down. You trust me, don't you, Josh? I'd never let anything bad happen to you, after all I am your guardian angel. So I'm going to get as close to you as possible. As you slowly stand up, keep your back pressed against the water tower and your eyes on me."

He did exactly what Gabby said. She was close enough to grab his hand. An instant calm washed over him. She continued to inch closer and closer to him until they were side by side."

She explained, "Now, Joshie, I'm going to put by arms around you, and you're going to close your eyes, and we're going to get off this water tower."

He didn't have time to argue. He felt slender arms encircle his hefty body. The thing he noticed first was the sound that came from behind him. It was a swooshing sound, loud and powerful. He tried to look behind him to see what was making that odd sound, but as soon as he did, his feet left the catwalk he was on, and he squeezed his eyes tightly shut. He had the oddest sensation of floating in the air, of being totally weightless. He would feel Gabby's arms wrapped tightly around him and hear the swooshing of mighty (dare he say it) of mighty wings. He couldn't see them, yet he instinctively knew that they were what was moving behind them as the two effortlessly floated to the ground below.

## Chapter Seventeen

As they touched the earth, Josh's eyes flew open, and he spun around to see Gabby standing behind him. "That was incredible! How did you do that?"

She didn't answer, just shrugged her shoulders with a smile on her face. Josh looked back up at the water tower and grabbed Gabby in a bear hug and swung her around. "Who cares how you did it, just thank you, thank you. I'm forever in your debt." He knew the truth of those words ran deep.

Gabby with her serene smile, nodded, and said, "Let's go home." She turned and headed for his truck. He hesitated for a moment. He didn't want this night to end so soon. He knew she was leaving. It would break his heart. He felt the tears well up in his eyes. He owed her so much. He glanced down at the ground where they had landed, and there was something white lying on the grass. He leaned down to pick it up, a feather, a beautifully shaped white feather shimmering in the moonlight. He smiled broadly and put the precious keepsake in his pants pocket. He followed Gabby to the truck.

On the ride home, they talked about many things. The urgency of time was upon them. Gabby reminded Josh of what to do on Monday morning and how he needed to be a friend that Jenna could depend on. He promised her that he would be that friend. They talked about secret things, things to come in the future, about the girl who would come, and how Josh would recognize her when the time was right. They talked about a life to be lived following the path God had planned and purposed before the beginning of time.

The boy and the angel stood at the backdoor of the Stewart home and said their goodbyes. Josh wishful that maybe she could stay a little longer; she reminding him that they would see each other again. Josh pulled the young angel to him and kissed her on the lips, a tender beautiful moment that he would never forget. Gabby standing there with that lovely smile on her face was a picture that would last him a lifetime.

He opened the door to go inside turning back for one final glance, but she was gone. He went down the driveway to look. Her car was gone too. He stood there looking up at all the stars twinkling in the night sky contemplating the awesomeness of God. He would be forever grateful for this brief encounter with the angel who had been sent from heaven just for him.

After he entered the house, he passed by Granny Bea's room without looking in on her; his heart was too heavy tonight. When he got to his room, he remembered the feather. He took it out of his pocket and placed it on his bedside table. Pristine white, perfectly shaped with a vibrant quality about it that glistened in the soft light, it lay there as a keepsake, a reminder of this unique time spent with his guardian angel. He would always cherish it and the memories of her. He lay on his bed thinking about all they had talked about before she left.

But someone else wasn't leaving without checking on the elderly woman down the hall. Gabby stood over her bed and kissed her gently on the forehead. Granny Bea's eyes opened slowly. She saw who stood over her.

*Chapter Seventeen*

"Is it my time, child. I'm ready to go."

Gabby shook her head, but reassured her. "Soon, Granny Bea, soon. I just wanted to let you know that Josh will be alright. No, better than that, he has a wonderful life ahead of him."

"Why sure enough, dear. I always knew God would answer my prayers. He sent you, didn't He?" Granny Bea chuckled to herself. "Will my angel come for me? The magnificent creature that saved me the night of the fire, will he come for me when it's my time?"

"Yes, Granny, your angel will come for you and bring you home. I'll be waiting with Al and Donnie to welcome you into heaven. Would you like that?"

Her frail body tensed with anticipation. Her face took on a slight glow as she thought about the homecoming that awaited her. "Thank you, Gabby dear. You were heaven sent and much appreciated. God is so good! I look forward to seeing you soon, and as we walk the streets of gold, you can tell me all about my Joshie's life. Will you do that, dear?"

"Yes, I will, anything for you, Granny Bea. Now goodnight." And she was gone.

# Chapter Eighteen

Gabby knelt before the throne of almighty God. His thundering voice was proclaiming throughout heaven, "WELL DONE MY GOOD AND FAITHFUL SERVANT! WELL DONE, MY ANGEL!"

The seraphim were circling His throne crying out, "Holy! Holy! Holy!"

Gabby also joined in the praises as she backed away from His pulsating energy and brilliant light. "Holy is the Lord God!" It was such an honor to stand before the One who always was, Alpha and Omega. To comprehend His majesty, His unlimited power, His infinite love was overwhelming for the young angel. Being in His presence and radiating in His glory was the place she wanted to be, but she had something she needed to do. How wonderful to serve Him and know that He was pleased with her were her thoughts as she backed away from His throne. Her feet barely touched the floor as she made her way across the sea of glass. She looked across the huge room to see Michael standing by the Room of Souls.

## Chapter Eighteen

He had a smile on his face and nodded his head to let her know he was pleased as well with the completion of her assignment. She briefly wondered about the next rolled parchment scroll he would hand her, but that would be for another time. As the heavy doors swung open for her, she stood face to face with the archangel Gabriel.

"So the little angel is back after another successful assignment. We all celebrate your success, Gabriella. You even managed to do more than what was required of you by helping the young girl. Very admirable to be sure! Father God is definitely pleased. There will be many more assignments for you, and I will be watching my little namesake with interest. Who knows, perhaps we will work together someday. Would you like that?"

Gabby, who had been struck mute by the majestic presence of the archangel, could only nod her head at the suggestion. He threw his head back and laughed at her inability to speak. He bowed ceremoniously and continued on his way.

The little angel now was free to search for Granny Bea's husband and son to let them know about her impending arrival. She wandered on the streets of gold that followed the river of life as it meandered through heaven. She saw Jesus among the people as usual. While Father God sat on His throne, His Son's one desire was to have fellowship with the saints. He knew their names. He walked with them, talked with them, and spent quality time with each and every one of them.

When He saw Gabby, He motioned for her to approach Him. While there was nothing about his appearance to make Him stand out in a crowd, as you approached Him, you instantly were aware of His identity because Jesus oozed loving-kindness and goodness. Pure love flowed from Him and gently wrapped around you like a living blanket. His eyes were warm and welcoming as He also congratulated her on a job well done.

He listened carefully as she explained her search and the reason for it. He knew exactly where to find the two she sought. He rejoiced that another family member would be reunited in heaven soon. It was the reason He went to earth and died such a cruel death on the cross so that all who believe could spend eternity with Him and Father God in heaven. He quickly sent the young angel on her way.

It didn't take her long to find them. As she approached them to introduce herself, she noticed a huge angel striding down the golden street with a look of purpose about him. She probably looked much the same way when she was on an assignment. She knew it had to be Granny Bea's guardian angel on his way to transport her from earth to her heavenly reward, an eternity with the One she believed in, prayed to and trusted, and the One who died to make it all possible. She smiled to think how happy Granny Bea would be to see her angel and finally make the journey to heaven. She shared the joyful news with Al and Donnie. There would be much joy and celebrating in heaven today, for another soul was coming home.

# Epilogue

Joshua Stewart had paced the floor of the delivery room all night. His parents had arrived in the early hours of the morning, but their first grandchild had not arrived yet. Josh's wife, April, had been a trooper as contractions wracked her body trying to push out this new life. He wasn't worried just tired. He knew it was a little girl trying so hard to be born. He and his wife were thrilled at the thought of being parents, and Josh was especially thrilled that his first child was a girl. He had let April quickly know that there would be only one consideration for her name. As a matter of fact, as he paced the floor, he had been thinking of his daughter's namesake and had taken the white feather out of his jacket pocket and gently rubbed it between his fingers. It made him feel better as if she was with him.

Josh was the youth pastor at the largest church in Whittleton. That's right, the hometown boy had stayed in his small town. He had gone away to college but soon realized the plan God had for his life, so he returned to build on the land that Granny Bea had left him. He had met April in college, knew immediately that she was the one he had been waiting for, and brought her back to Whittleton. They had been married for several years, and he loved her dearly. He was close to his parents, who were very proud of him and the job he was doing with the local youth. He was working with a lot of kids whose parents were his own friends back during his high school days. Funny how life had come full circle, and he was helping kids the way Gabby had helped him face his own fears and problems. He loved his job and was very grateful for the rewarding, blessed life he had.

Thinking about high school made him think of Jenna. He had been seated next to her as she told her story to the principal that morning so long ago. Both of them had to stay strong during the investigation that followed and the fallout for those involved. When things were tough, they only had to remember a certain smiling face and the words of encouragement she had spoken to them. Drawing from that strength, Jenna had fought her way back from the evil that tried to destroy her. It hadn't been easy, and it didn't happen overnight. But she had triumphed. She lived in a different state, and was a counselor now, working with girls whose past mirrored her own. She had a husband and two kids. Through the years, she and Josh had kept in touch. He would call her later and tell her about the new addition to his family.

He thought about Kyle as well. The last time he had seen his friend was on that Monday, when he and Jenna told the principal and then the police about the events of that fateful Saturday night. Kyle had

*Epilogue*

been arrested and sent to a juvenile facility where apparently he went from bad to worse. The last time Josh heard anything about his old friend was that he was serving fifteen years in a federal prison for drug trafficking.

April's family finally arrived from out of town, and it was time for this baby to come forth. Josh's reminiscing was interrupted as the nurse called for him to join his wife as they welcomed the birth of their daughter.

Later the proud dad brought the tiny infant out into the waiting room to meet her grandparents. "Let me introduce you to Miss Gabriella Beatrice Stewart, but we'll be calling her Gabby."

He had a smile from ear to ear, and he bet several people in heaven did too! Could life get any better!

Visit friendsforeverbook.com

CPSIA information can be obtained at www.ICGtesting.com
Printed in the USA
LVOW07s0226170516

488550LV00001B/2/P